A Journey

into

Spiritual Healing

and

Kirlian Photography

A down to earth approach
to
Hands on Healing

David Clements

*Written by a practising spiritual healer and teacher for
those starting out on their own healing journey.*

BALBOA.
PRESS
A DIVISION OF HAY HOUSE

Balboa Press books may be ordered through booksellers or by contacting:

Balboa Press
A Division of Hay House
1663 Liberty Drive
Bloomington, IN 47403
www.balboapress.com.au
1-(877) 407-4847

ISBN: 978-1-4525-1159-7 (sc)
ISBN: 978-1-4525-1160-3 (e)

Because of the dynamic nature of the Internet, any web addresses or links contained in
this book may have changed since publication and may no longer be valid. The views
expressed in this work are solely those of the author and do not necessarily reflect the
views of the publisher, and the publisher hereby disclaims any responsibility for them.

The author of this book does not dispense medical advice or prescribe the use of any
technique as a form of treatment for physical, emotional, or medical problems without the
advice of a physician, either directly or indirectly. The intent of the author is only to offer
information of a general nature to help you in your quest for emotional and spiritual well-
being. In the event you use any of the information in this book for yourself, which is your
constitutional right, the author and the publisher assume no responsibility for your actions.

Balboa Press rev. date: 09/18/2013

Acknowledgements

Sincere thanks to my family and friends who have helped me and shown interest in what I am doing, with special thanks to my friends Lee and Marilyn for their interest in this book, and their expertise on the computer during many hours spent putting it together.

Dedicated to those friends, helpers and loved ones in the world of Spirit who have helped and guided me, who have shown utmost patience with me during our journey, and who lifted me up when I fell.

Picture 1. A proud moment for me when in 1989 I was made a Practising Healer member of The National Federation of Spiritual Healers.

Spiritual Healing

is

a Spiritual Act and Love

is

the Force that Motivates

it

The power

that made the body

can heal the body

JESUS looked at them and said: "There are some things that people can't do, but God can do anything."—MARK 10:27

Contents

Foreword

David Clements has written this book from his varied experiences when developing his potential as a spiritual healer. He has done so against great odds, and the book should help to ease the way of those who read it and choose to follow in his footsteps.

He has written an introduction to healing from the viewpoint of a Spiritualist. He therefore lays emphasis on the role of spirit guardians, guides and helpers, an angle that some writers would over look, relating directly to the source.

David's path to writing *A Journey into Spiritual Healing and Kirlian Photography* has been guided, but has required grit and determination on his part to reach his goal, to fulfil his aim.

For those who happen to live in the U.K. the path is much easier. Healing is widely accepted and scarcely ridiculed. The statement, "I am a spiritual healer" usually gives rise to interested questions rather than scathing criticism, or fear of the devil's work, from the listener. The media shows a positive interest, many medics cooperate and even some church ministers react favourably.

In David's case it has been more difficult, as it is for healers in the United States, Canada and many parts of Europe. Australia is a big country. Healers in many areas are isolated and in order to link with people who hold similar beliefs he has had to rely on people like myself who live far away.

David and I have been friends for about eight years and during that time numerous airmail letters have passed between us. Networking has been invaluable and determination and faith have kept him on task.

The book is written in a personal and easy to read style. There are no frills or fancy trimmings; it is down to earth, like its author; written for down to earth people.

The National Federation of Spiritual Healers has been mentioned several times as a role model to follow. It has taken over 40 years for enthusiastic volunteers to build it into a thriving and highly respected organisation with about 1,600 members in England and overseas. Several staff members are paid to keep it running efficiently and smoothly. It is non-denominational so that people of many different faiths work under its banner. The standards of training are high, as are the requirements for entry into membership. Attached to membership is comprehensive insurance, valid providing that the member abides by the strong Code of Conduct. The NFSH gives an assurance of quality, respectability and professionalism to the public.

David Clements is a dedicated Full Healer Member of the National Federation of Spiritual Healers, with a genuine interest to share the knowledge he has gained over the years.

Read on. Decide whether you want to develop your own healing potential and then go ahead and do it!

Shirley Brooker

Vice President, National Federation of Spiritual Healers from 1991 to 1994

National Chairwoman from 1994 to 1996

1

Preamble

I have written this book to try to help people who are interested in spiritual healing understand that they also have the ability to heal. One need not spend lots of money on very expensive courses in order to become a healer, for it is your God-given right and part of your spiritual destiny. My belief in spirit guides and helpers and my understanding that we are part of a 'Big Plan' that is guided by spirit has been proved to me on numerous occasions. I accept totally that I am used as a channel for healing energy to flow through, and that the healings are performed by a higher intelligence than me. At certain times in the book I have repeated what I consider important points for you to grasp and accept. I hope that you will enjoy the book and trust that it will be of help to you on your journey.

This book on Healing has not been written in one session; it has been put together over about 24 months or so. During this time I have been offered advice on how it should be done. Mostly, may I say, by people unskilled in book writing or publishing. I am sure that people have been well meaning in their advice and I thank them for caring.

One suggestion that was made to me was put this way: "David, the word 'Spiritual' is not commercial, not sellable; it sounds too religious. Some Healers are refraining from using it, along with all references to spirit guides or helpers, on the basis that it sounds to most people to be supernatural or psychic, and won't be accepted by people out there who buy books." I thanked the person concerned for this advice and naturally considered the situation.

Please bear with me, for I wish to express what is in my heart and hope that you can understand: I was born under the sign of Virgo. I am very down to earth, sceptical and not easily convinced. I was told early on in my life that I was to be 'a healer', which I did not understand. Once I became involved in a small way in healing I was, can I say, introduced to my spirit guides. As I became more committed, these spirit helpers told me certain situations that would occur in my life. All turned out 100% true. I was informed that these spirit people had been with me in previous incarnations, and are with me during my life here on earth. We have work to do, both now and in the future, and I pray that I may be able to develop and use whatever abilities I have to be of service.

I know that it is not I who am responsible for any healings which take place. I know how much Spirit influences things in our lives and I understand that we are part of the plan for what is to be our future. I know that Spirit has been influential in my life, not running my life or doing it for me, but guiding and directing me.

I feel so sorry for those people who think otherwise and especially those who believe that it is they who are responsible for healings which take place.

For what is Faith? It is to believe in that which we cannot see!

We shall all know the truth in the not too distant future.

I have the courage of my convictions; I have used the title, and shall continue to call myself a spiritual healer, and I shall always give credit where it is due, to those loving, caring souls in the Spirit Realm, who work with us spiritual healers in this physical world, to serve mankind.

I hope to be able to use revenue from book sales to advance the cause of spiritual healing in whatever way I can, maybe to establish a sanctuary where no charge would be made for healing. This would enable many to be helped. I would see the Sanctuary also as a place for people to be trained in the healing arts, and where they would be able to practise and develop their healing abilities. I have a mental picture of what could be achieved, and invite suggestions from interested persons.

I hope also to be able to make a financial donation to the National Federation of Spiritual Healers, to thank them and to help them to continue the great work that they are doing to practice and promote spiritual healing.

Scientific research throughout history has shown us how the world operates on the material level. Many healings which have occurred, due to Prayer, Distant Healing or laying on of hands are, by scientific principles, *impossible*! Yet they have happened!

Surely this must show that there is a higher intelligence at work here, which is not physical.

I send my love to that band of spiritual healers in the Spirit World who is bound to me and me to them, and thank them for being so patient and unselfish. Loving and caring for me when I'm sure it could have been easier for them to walk away and to find another channel, much easier than I, to work with.

There is no one school of thought which can provide all the answers for us on matters spiritual (psychic). No one has a monopoly on the truth, despite what some people or some groups tell us, insisting that theirs alone is the right way. Each of us creates our own perception of what the truth is; it must feel comfortable to us, and be in harmony with our inner feelings, our intuition. Even scientists themselves concede that there are many things which they have to accept, but which they cannot prove.

The trust and faith in spiritual healing and spiritual ideas involves a personal and inborn belief; it is impossible to accept and practise spiritual principles without such a strong belief. These principles cannot really be tested or proven, and must therefore be accepted. I feel that we need to listen and rely more on what our heart is telling us than the thoughts that are coming from our head. As we go forward on our journey let us resolve to show love and compassion to those that we may meet on the way.

Visiting London from Australia on my quest to learn more about spiritual healing, I was thrilled to be asked by the National Federation organisers to work as a healer on their stand at this prestigious exhibition. It was wonderful for me to be on the stand and to meet members of the public who came on to the stand to ask questions so that they could learn more about healing. Working with other healers also broadens one's knowledge and provides opportunities to discuss aspects of healing. It was whilst I was working on the stand that I met Shirley Brooker, a wonderful lady who was so helpful and considerate. Shirley is devoted to her healing work and spends much of her time helping people like myself to progress their healing work. We are still good friends to this day and correspond on a regular basis, which is very beneficial to me. I look back on those days with much happiness and thank those people like Shirley for the fond memories.

Picture 2. The N.F.S.H. stand at the Mind, Body, and Spirit Exhibition in London in 1989. One can see the huge interest in Healing by the amount of people participating.

Picture 3. One of the fund raising days that we held. These were a good way for us as healers to get our message over to the general public. Everybody gave their time for free and a good time was had by all. This type of function is ideal for healers to get confidence in dealing with the public. Probationary healers can learn useful techniques that will enhance their healing and counselling skills. People who come along are able to experience hands on healing and ask questions in a friendly atmosphere.

2

Spiritual Healing

In the rapidly changing world in which we live, we are seeing many changes on a global scale. It is as if there is a speeding up, a quickening of the pace of change.

Who in their wildest dreams would have thought that we would see the fall of communism in Russia and the pulling back of troops from East Berlin, East and West Germany re-uniting after 50 years of being virtual enemies, the changes in South Africa (which now has a black President) and an end to apartheid in that country?

Who would have imagined Israel and the Palestinians signing peace treaties, and the I.R.A. in Northern Ireland declaring a truce after so many years of senseless killings and violence. Does it not make you wonder, and ask yourself, is something going on that we can't see? I believe that there is, and that it is our spirit friends who are at work here.

When one has been involved with, worked for, and believes what Spirit is capable of, it is no surprise to us. We can understand it to be part of Spirit's 'Big Plan'. This is why I call spiritual healing the 'Therapy of the Future'.

We shall all play our part as spiritual healers in 'God's Plan for Earth'.

The Time is fast approaching.

3

Setting the Scene

When I began writing this book I realised that it would not be possible to relate every experience that has happened in my life, so I have tried to condense a very full life into a relatively brief story, which I hope will hold your interest. I feel sure that many of you will relate to it, for there will be incidents or situations with which you will feel some empathy. Spirit has told me that I chose a hard path to walk this time and they haven't been wrong, I can tell you. I wonder sometimes what sort of person I was in previous lives to have chosen this one in an effort to make amends and to get myself on the right path again, and so help my spiritual development.

No mortal of woman born, can shun their destiny.

I do hope that you enjoy the book and that it will help you on your path through life and trust that it will all come together for you, when the time is right for you!

The journey of a thousand miles begins with the first step.

Take that step and keep on going forward.

Good Luck and God Bless.

David

4

My Story, to which you may Relate!

I would like to tell you a little more about myself and how I came to write this book. I hope that you find it interesting and I am sure that many of you will relate to some of the events that I have experienced.

I was born in South London and in my early childhood I spent quite a lot of time with my grandmother who lived in the country away from London and the bombing of World War II. Recollections of my childhood are very vague so I shall jump to my teenage years. I left Buckhurst Hill Country High School in Essex in my mid-teens with virtually no academic qualifications; I was a poor scholar.

I always had an interest in such things as ghosts, U.F.O.s, ouija boards and things in this area. I completed my National Service with the 1st Royal Tank Regiment in Germany and returned to civilian life and the search for a career.

This was an unsettling time for me and when my younger brother decided to emigrate to Australia, I gave this some thought, and after much soul-searching I also decided to emigrate to Perth in Western Australia.

My first impression on arriving in Perth was wanting to go straight back to London, which at that time seemed to be the centre of the world, whereas Perth was like a small country town. I had to stay 2 years anyway and after meeting up with my brother and finding a job I did settle OK.

I still had this interest in what I shall call 'the psychic' and often visited Spiritualist churches, where many times I was given a message. I only had an interest, but really very little knowledge or understanding, so when I was told that I should be doing the work, I really didn't know what that meant. As time went on I got involved with a group which used to meet every Monday evening to meditate for development. I attended this group for about 12 months. I heard nothing and saw nothing, whilst others in the group did. So I became quite disenchanted and said to the leader of the group, "Look, I think I shall give this a miss, I'm not getting anywhere and I'm probably holding others back."

"Oh, don't do that," she said, "you are the powerhouse for all the energy we use." So I did carry on until the circle broke up.

Around about this time my cousin Penny emigrated to Perth from London and together we joined a group and started our own circle, which was led by a man who was a direct voice medium, with what purported to be Spirit voices speaking through him. At first this seemed to be really what we had all been looking for, but unfortunately it became more and more evident that his motives were not the best and he was using whatever gift he had for his own ends and to the detriment of others close to him.

We parted company under unpleasant circumstances and both my cousin Penny and I were left wondering if we were on the right track. We did a lot of soul searching and felt totally let down by Spirit—lots of questions but no answers. We didn't know what to do or where to go. Why was this deceit allowed to happen to us? Was it some sort of test for us, maybe to make us more perceptive of the people we were working with? It was at this time that Penny told me that before she left London she had several clairvoyant readings with a well known London medium who told her that someone close to her in her family was a very strong healer, with much healing ability. Penny's clairvoyance was getting stronger but because of family commitments she decided for the time being to stop. It was at this time she advised me that I was the person mentioned in her readings as a healer who would go on to do much work in this field.

I half-heartedly went along to Spiritualist churches, even though I felt let down by Spirit for all the deceit that had gone on. I wanted answers to many questions and I was not getting them. Still the messages came when I visited the Churches, although now they mentioned healing and the fact that I was a healer. I can remember having healing at a Spiritualist church and the healer saying, "Your hands are so hot. It is you who should be giving healing to me."

What was this healing I used to ask myself. What do you do? What's it all about? Seemingly no one could tell me, or wanted to, in Perth at that time—so I was left wondering.

I truly cannot say like so many others in this work that I saw or heard things from childhood because I just didn't, even though I did want to. I wasn't given messages or directions from spirit guides and so it made me feel very inadequate. I felt that I was stumbling along on my own, not really knowing where I was going or what I was doing. I had no one to turn to, to ask questions on healing, etc., and when my cousin asked me if I could help her best friend's baby, I didn't know what to do. The baby, whose name was also David, was born with a lump on his head. Not a deformity, but to do with the birth. Of course the mother Joan was upset, and the Nursing Staff had told her it was all right, and that because a baby's head is soft when born the lump will gradually go down, until it goes completely. I was at a loss to know what to do, so I placed my hands on the baby's head and said a prayer and asked desperately for help. Two days later Penny rang me at work and said that Joan had been back to the hospital and that the lump had totally gone.

The Nursing Sister said, "This couldn't happen; are you sure its the same baby? I've never heard of this before."

A close friend in the family, who suffered severe migraines and had to take a tablet every day, asked me if I could do anything for him. Again I thought, "What do I do?" I felt lost and inadequate. But I did lay my hands on his head and said a prayer for help, adding a special plea because I felt out of my depth here. Bert decided after this to stop taking the tablets and to this day has not had a bad migraine attack. How wonderful, but I still didn't understand it and had even more questions, and there was no one who I could really ask to obtain the knowledge I so desperately needed.

I was reading more and more books and the one which impressed me most was by the great English healer, Harry Edwards. After reading his story and his life's plan, I knew I had found what I could call 'my hero'. Here was a man who had actually done the things I could only dream about. I was so taken by the wonderful way in which he taught that healing should be, so basic and straightforward, it was incredible. I knew this was the way I wanted to develop.

Many of the books one reads on spiritual healing are written by people who have not actually healed, but Harry Edwards had proven his theories. He had accomplished what he believed, not just talked about it. My understanding of healing and the way it is done took a great leap forward. For the first time I really understood that I was being used by 'spirit forces', who were so much more knowledgeable than I was. I came to understand that I was merely a channel for this energy to flow through. I continued to search for knowledge and had this sort of inner urge to develop whatever abilities I had, yet not really knowing how to go about it.

It was about this time that I was to go through the worst period of my life. My family split up and I lost my business and partnership with my brother. I was also being embezzled by two sisters on my staff who took me and the business for thousands. Sadly my trust was badly abused. Through the trauma and emotional stress of losing family, business and friends, my own self-esteem plummeted. I went from a successful businessman with family, future and financial security, to being unemployed, devastated, not knowing what to do, and feeling that there was only myself to blame. My confidence was gone and I felt ill. I couldn't sleep and had no direction of where to go or what to do. Some friends and family deserted me and some helped me get through it with their support.

To try to get some direction, I consulted a clairvoyant who didn't know me or anything about me. As we sat in her house having a coffee, she said to me, "You've had a pretty tough time lately, haven't you?"

Not wanting to tell her too much, I said, "You could say that."

She then said, "I'm being told it was all meant to happen."

"You've got to be joking," I replied.

"No," she said. "How many times have you been told, you should be doing the work?"

"All the time," I said.

"And you haven't been doing it, have you? So they have taken all your toys away."

I couldn't believe it. I had thought that Spirit were my friends, there to help me.

I was devastated, I went away and thought about all that had happened to me and what I had been told. I started to see things more clearly. Yes, I was a 'Gunna'! I was always 'going to do it' but never did.

People said to me "How come you never had a breakdown, with all that happened to you?" I think I know who helped me to get through it all. I believe that those close to me in the Spirit world helped me through my devastation, for they had work for me to do. The gift of healing I possessed was part of my destiny and was to be used to help others in this world who needed healing. But I had to learn a very valuable lesson and, by gee, I did.

My mother and stepfather helped me greatly and I did, after much application and many interviews, get a sales consultant position. This led on to another and then another job, during which time I built up my self-esteem, confidence and my bank balance.

During the next period I was still searching for that elusive knowledge and getting my life in more order, spending time with my two children, Sharon and Mark. I always had that inner urge, it is like a drug—you can't give it up, its always there—something you can't describe, yet you alone feel. I'm sure many people reading this book will have experienced the same feeling.

Things were going along quite well, I thought, when one morning I awoke with an ache in my arm and pain in my right hand. I couldn't shave or hold a pen to write a letter; it was a constant ache all the time, with a numbness and pins and needles. I went to doctors, physiotherapists, to hospital for a scan, but all I could find out was that it was a pinched nerve in my neck area. No one could help me, and it was very debilitating. After several months of getting nowhere, I was prompted to write to the Harry Edwards Healing Sanctuary in England to ask for absent healing. I took a photograph, put my condition/complaint in writing on the back and asked for help. I sent it off and forgot about it.

About a week passed and it was still there. Then one morning I got up, went into the bathroom and suddenly realised that the pain had gone, and my fingers were no longer numb. It was like I had to walk on eggshells, I was so careful not to jerk or do anything too quickly, lest it returned.

Several days later a letter arrived from the Harry Edwards Sanctuary saying that from such and such a date they had instigated absent healing for me. That was the day my pain and numbness disappeared. You can call it coincidence or what you like, but I know it could only have been one thing—Spirit had helped me and showed me what they could do, when all else, including conventional medical treatments, had failed.

I do believe, and I had it confirmed later, that I needed to endure this pain to teach me a lesson; that if I had this gift of healing then I should be using it to help people in pain—I guess I'm just a slow learner.

It was just after this that I changed jobs and went into the real estate industry, listing and selling houses. I was very lucky because when I started to work it was at the beginning of a boom period which was to last about two years. I enjoyed the work even though the hours were quite long. I still maintained my interest in psychic matters and became good friends with a lady who was a clairvoyant. I liked her approach to it, for she was very honest and down to earth, and we used to sit and discuss all manner of interesting things. All was going quite well until Christmas 1988 when suddenly the real estate business fell very flat. Suddenly things were not too good for salesmen as we were on a commission only basis: no sales, no pay.

My income dropped drastically and I said to my clairvoyant friend, Marlene, that I thought I would get a regular job, one which paid me a weekly wage. Her comment was, "You won't get one until you have done what you should do." All during this period I still had the urge to know more about 'this healing thing'. It was always there, inside. It wouldn't go away.

People would ask me questions about healing; I would pick up books in the library about healing; it was as if it was being put in front of me all the time.

Again, I ignored what Marlene told me and went off in pursuit of this envisioned job. I applied for four positions and in each case narrowly missed out. One prospective employer even said he needed to choose between myself, and another ideal candidate, and that we were both what he was looking for.

"I shall have to toss a coin," he said.

Well here goes, I thought, my Spirit friends will look after me now; its in the bag. Guess what! Yes, I missed out again. Again, Marlene said to me, "You have to do what you know you should be doing."

Things weren't working; I wasn't selling any houses. I wandered into the local travel agent and enquired about fares to the United Kingdom. The girl was very helpful and gave me brochures, and then said, "Why don't you take a round the world trip? its only another $300.00 and is valid for a year."

I took the details home with me and thought it over, the points for, and the ones against. It seemed a big risk to take, a journey into the unknown; would it be successful, was it the best thing to do, where would I make for? No, I didn't know anyone over there. What happens if it doesn't work out? Think of all that money wasted.

So I virtually talked myself out of it. Isn't it funny how when we analyse things, we seem to go towards the negative. So by Monday I had just about abandoned the idea and put it to one side.

The phone rang on my desk, it was the travel agent. "Mr Clements, just to advise you that there is to be a fare rise, so if you want to go please book your seat. You don't have to pay for it till later. I shall wait to hear from you."

"OK, book me on for the end of March," the words came out. What was I saying? It was done, and somehow I felt a weight lifted off my shoulders. I resigned my job, prepared to leave my home unit, and started to plan. During a clairvoyant reading, I was told that I would meet an older man, who would take me under his wing and would be a great help to me. I was reassured that my trip would be worthwhile.

Before leaving I visited several of the Spiritualist churches, one of whom gave me a nice reference attesting to my healing ability, which I took with me, along with several references from patients I had helped. I left Perth for London via Kuala Lumpur. When I arrived in London Airport my baggage was missing. I was told that it was still in Kuala Lumpur, but would be delivered to me at my cousin's house in Cambridge. Off I go into the arrival area to meet my cousin, who was to pick me up. I looked around but no cousin and no message for me. I rang his house and his wife said, "The clutch has broken on the car; he can't come to pick you up."

I'm standing there in my shorts, thongs and T-shirt with my hand luggage, Australian style in the middle of London Airport wondering, "Is Spirit trying to tell me something." Maybe I shouldn't be here, no baggage, no lift! I took the underground train to Liverpool Street Station and caught the train up to Cambridge. I must have looked a real twit. Here I was in my shorts and T-shirt, whilst everyone else was dressed much more for the weather. Having 'Australia' blazoned across the front of my shirt, people must have thought I was a bit eccentric. When I got to Cambridge it was raining, and as I walked along the platform a couple of ladies behind me said, "He's not dressed for this sort of weather, is he."

Three days later my baggage arrived and I went off to Stanstead Hall to try to book into a course at the Academy there. I booked in to a course called "How Spirit Works". Whilst I was there I called in to see the secretary of the Spiritualist National Union, a major Spiritualist church group in England and Australia. I had a reference from one of their Reverends to show him of my work in Australia. The guy I spoke to was a bit perplexed after I explained to him that I had worked in Churches in Perth and was here to further my education in relation to healing, and I was seeking contacts who could help me.

"We can't let you go into our Churches to do healing," he said.

"Why not," I asked, "I only want to work with some of your people, so that I can learn. Here is a reference from one of your own church Reverends."

"You haven't spent all that money coming to England to learn healing, have you?" he asked me.

"As a matter of fact, I have," I said.

"Well, we cannot help you—try some of the other groups," he said as he showed me the door.

Driving back to Cambridge, the thoughts were coming thick and fast and things weren't looking very promising. First my baggage mix-up, second, no one to meet me at the airport, and now this major snub. Was Spirit trying to tell me something, I wondered.

I left Cambridge and drove down to London to look up an Aunt on my father's side, who lived in South East London. I met with a good reception; she was pleased to see me and agreed to put me up for a while. I then decided to go over to the other side of London to call on The National Federation of Spiritual Healers at their headquarters. During the journey, I kept wondering what I would do if they couldn't or wouldn't assist me.

On arrival I sat in the car and asked for help, plucked up courage and walked in. I explained what my mission was and the staff were very helpful and asked me to wait awhile until the lady they felt could advise me was available. I was called into the office and was introduced to Audrey Murr-Copland, who made me feel very welcome and asked how she could help. I explained my wish to learn more about spiritual healing and that I had come from Western Australia to do so. Audrey explained how their group could help me. It sounded great! I was then signed up as a Probationary Healer and completed all the necessary paperwork. Audrey asked where I was lodging, so I told her I was in Sydenham.

"The best person for you to contact," she said, "is Ron Broadbent; he runs the healing clinic in Bromley. That is very near where you are staying in Sydenham but, as it is a long way from here, he rarely comes into the office. I'll give you his phone number, for you to ring him to make arrangements."

Whilst waiting for receipts and literature, I had a look around the Bookshop. I suppose some 20-30 minutes went by, and then Audrey called me into the office.

"I would like you to meet Ron Broadbent," she said, and introduced me to the tall gentleman standing there. This was very good timing—was it just coincidence?

I Spoke to Ron and explained my situation. He was most helpful and outlined to me how the Bromley Clinic worked and made me feel very pleased to be able to join the staff. I made arrangements to attend the following week. I knew intuitively that this was the man I was destined to meet, for I had been told by Spirit prior to my leaving Perth that I would be 'looked after'. This was further proof of it.

Over the next few months of my stay in England, Ron was to be a great help to me in my settling in process, and my development as a spiritual healer. He really did take me under his wing (as had been predicted) and was instrumental in so many ways towards furthering my development as a Spiritual Healer. I owe Ron Broadbent my deepest and heartfelt gratitude for being so caring and helpful. "Thank you Ron." Yet Audrey had said he never goes into the office. Could it be coincidence? Or could it have been Spirit guiding me?

I started working as a spiritual healer at the Bromley Healing Centre, to do my probation. All the healers were wonderful to me and helped me immensely, and my thanks go out to them all. Ron kept an eye on me and offered good advice, and my working with the other Healers was giving me excellent tutelage and experience. It wasn't long before Ron told me that he felt I was quite capable of working on my own with clients. I really did relish this opportunity and it was most rewarding to hear that clients often asked to see 'that Aussie guy'. During this time I attended the Basic Healing Course and the Advanced Healing Course conducted by the N.F.S.H. I now was headed in the right direction, gaining practice at the Bromley Centre and a period of time at Farnborough Hospital Centre.

I was so proud to be asked to work on the N.F.S.H. stand at the prestigious 'Mind, Body and Spirit' exhibition and the 'Here's Health' exhibition. It was a great thrill for me to be part of this promotional campaign to meet the general public. I worked each day of both exhibitions from opening to closing. it's not every day one has an opportunity to do this, and I loved every minute of it. It was so nice to meet such lovely people, both healers and the public, and I was gaining so much valuable experience, in every way.

On the final night of the 'Mind, Body and Spirit Expo' the lady healer I was working with suddenly said, "You have a Red Indian standing by your right shoulder. He is smiling and looks very happy." I knew who it was and thanked him for being with me. It was very reassuring to know he was there.

Sometime later I was invited to tea at the home of one of my healer friends. I had chosen this particular day to call in at the airline office to arrange my passage from London to New York. I was running out of money and this was worrying me. Also I was going through a period of inner turmoil, so all in all I was feeling quite dissatisfied and upset. When I arrived at my friend's home, we sat and had a drink and I told her I expected to be leaving London shortly on my way back to Australia.

She looked at me as if she was looking past me and said, "Your Indian Friend is here and he doesn't want you to leave yet."

Because of the mood I was in I snapped back, "Too bad! I have had enough of it all, so I'm heading back home."

"He understands your anger. You are being tested again," she replied.

"I am sick to death of tests, it never stops," I replied.

"He is asking you to be patient, for if you stay it will benefit you."

By this time I had calmed down, so I said, "I'm sick of being patient, but thank him and please tell him I will stay on."

I believe my staying did benefit me in several ways, the most important for me and my healing credibility was that thanks to my dear friend Ron Broadbent I was made a full healer member of the National Federation of Spiritual Healers, which is to me the highest public honour a healer can achieve.

I eventually left England and crossed the Atlantic to America and stayed and worked for a short period in Los Angeles with Sarah Stephenson, who was quite well known there as a spiritual healer. I would have loved to have stayed longer in America but my finances were nearly gone so I flew back to Australia and home base.

I arrived back in Perth, Western Australia in September 1989. I had no job and no where to live, so I stayed with my mother and slept on the couch. I had learnt much and had a lot of ideas and information on spiritual healing. On my first visit to the Spiritualist Church I was totally ignored. My second visit was the same. I felt I had much I could impart to them, but was advised in a round about way that I wasn't wanted. It is sad to see that people's egos don't let them 'practice what they preach'. I contacted another local Psychic Development Group regarding joining up with a healing group and was told that they were very cliquey and didn't exactly welcome outsiders with open arms. She suggested that my recent enriching London experience with the N.F.S.H. wouldn't exactly help my cause either. Because I knew more than they did about spiritual healing I wouldn't be welcome in the group. Funny isn't it, we all work for God, yet it seems we cannot work together. One despairs of humans.

A friend suggested that we form our own group and run a healing course and see what happened from there. This we did and out of that first course we formed a band of healers and opened our first healing centre at a hall in Warwick, a suburb of Perth. It was the first such centre where people could come for healing and also where probationary healers could practice and hone their skills. This ran for 2 years and resulted in many success stories.

It is particularly difficult to achieve a greater public understanding and acceptance of spiritual healing in this country, particularly here in Western Australia.

When I returned and appraised the field with renewed eyes and heart, my first reaction was to turn on my heels and fly back to England, where spiritual healing is widely accepted. However I was told in no uncertain terms by Spirit that I was here to break new ground and to pioneer the way. I interested a journalist from our local sunday newspaper who came out and did a story, which showed us in a very good light. Unfortunately the editor's attitude was 'I am not pushing the boat out for Spiritual Healing'. How can a person with such a closed mind manage to get a job like he has?

Because we worked on a donation only basis, we did not have big money to spend on promotion, unlike some of the other therapies which are far more commercial and money orientated.

Consequently most people get to hear about Spiritual Healing through word of mouth, which is a slower process, though a surer one. There have been changes of location of the healing centres but the work has continued.

It was whilst I was receiving healing from Carol, a friend and fellow healer, that my Red Indian guide showed himself and spoke through her to me. He spoke of our connection with the White Brotherhood, and that we are part of the Big Plan, and are what he calls chosen ones. Being very inquisitive, I asked if we would see great healings achieved in the future, like those facilitated by the great English healer Harry Edwards. My guide responded, "what you term as miracles today, in time to come will be every day occurrences, as you will not have the medical facilities that you do have now." We have over time had many sessions with him and the one thing I wish I could share with you is that tremendous emotional feeling you get when he simply says, "We love you". It brings a lump to one's throat.

It is 'Love' which is always emphasised by our spirit friends. They emphasise too that it is our needs, the basic items in life, which are met, and not our desires. When Carol asked my guide if our spirit friends ever found me difficult to work with, due to my down to earth attitude, his comment was, "Well, we get frustrated but we never give up. You see, we know him," and he gave a sigh!

As I have a very down to earth attitude towards most matters, I am told that I don't match many people's preconception of what a spiritual healer should be like. I tend to see life's issues as very black and white, perhaps because I have a natal sun in Virgo, with Virgo rising. Throw in a strong streak of scepticism and a compulsion to prove things, and it becomes apparent that the path of a spiritual healer is not one that is inherently an easy one for me to tread. Quite frankly though, when one is involved in alternative or complementary therapies, it never ceases to amaze me what some people will do to make a dollar. Some of the names they can think up for a therapy are amazing. A massage becomes a biodynamic massage. Healing becomes magnified to 'cosmic' healing. It would appear that some practitioners need to give their therapy an air of mysticism to attract people to them. Yet there seem to be plenty of vulnerable people out there who have money to spend. Is it any wonder that the medical profession throw their hands up in shock when someone does a six week course in something, and then becomes an instant expert and sets up business. There are also the others who pay lots of money to do courses and then pay up even more money and become a 'Master'.

It is my belief that there is only one source of healing energy, and this energy, coming from its Divine source and channelled/directed by a higher intelligence (our spirit friends) is responsible for all healing.

The power that made the body can heal the body.

I asked my spirit friend about this. The reply was that there are no Masters in our world: every aspect of Spiritual/Psychic development has to be earned, whether it be in a previous incarnation or this life. 'Develop the humility and lose the ego.'

For spiritual healing to be accepted as a therapy of integrity, I believe that the way ahead must be for us all to strive for credibility, and to prove to the medical profession that we are genuine and credible in what we do.

He who loses credibility can lose nothing more.

We must have better training for our healers so that we can offer an improved service. I would like to see our healers of the future obtaining some knowledge of orthodox medicine. More training in counselling and listening skills would also be a great advantage to all healers. The National Federation of Spiritual Healers has made tremendous progress towards better training for our healers. The very fact of the federation's policy of spiritual healing being complementary to orthodox medicine should enable us to work together, so that we can show people by the way we act, and by the results that can be obtained, that we are indeed becoming the 'Therapy of the Future.'

5

A History of Spiritual Healing

Spiritual healing has been on earth from the time that the first humans appeared. As we are a spirit in a body, so the early humans were spirits taking on earthly form. As far back in history as it is possible to trace man's development, spiritual healing has played its part. It is most certainly not something that has just recently been discovered. Where do we start? One can imagine those early cave people sitting around on the ground in front of the caves they lived in. Most likely they looked up at the night sky and the millions of stars twinkling in the heavens and thought, "What am I doing here? What happens when I die? What is it all about?" Questions we are still asking today.

We can deduce that primitive man had some belief in an afterlife, for we know that they didn't just leave their dead to rot on the ground for animals to eat. They buried their dead with their weapons and personal possessions, suggesting that the dead person would need them wherever they went.

It is quite possible that these early tribes did worship some kind of spirit power and would thus have had a person in the tribe with some sort of power or knowledge of the healing arts.

We can now come forward in time many thousands of years, during which time mankind evolved greatly, to the early civilisations of ancient Egypt, the builders of the Pyramids. Fortunately the ancient Egyptians have left records written down which give us a revealing insight into the life that they lived and their beliefs.

The High Priest of that day was a very powerful influence on the Pharaohs of that time. He was well versed in religious as well as medical wisdom, and totally believed in an after-life. Once again we see that the Pharaohs were mummified and buried with jewels and personal possessions. Even their servants were slain and buried along with them, demonstrating their belief in life continuing, in some form or other, after physical death. There is evidence that suggests the Egyptian High Priests regarded spiritual healing as a very powerful therapy and we know that they established schools where novice priests were taught the healing arts.

As one civilisation declined, so another sprang up to take its place. It is around the temple of Aesculapius that we see healing progressing and the development of medicine as the embryo of what we know today.

Aesculepius was famous for his powers of healing and was deified as the Greek god of medicine. Possibly the most celebrated physician of antiquity, Hippocrates, was born in Greece and his emblem, the serpent and staff, is the emblem of the medical profession today.

As we move through time and the different civilisations, each with their belief in the Spirit and an after-life we come to the Roman Empire. The Romans were a warlike society, more advanced in many ways than others that had gone before. They suppressed other states and imposed their own religions and beliefs on the people.

It was during this period that there was born, in Nazareth in Judaea, a person who was to further the cause of spiritual healing like no one before or after him. We talk now of Jesus Christ, born of a poor carpenter in a town under Roman rule. Speculation abounds as to where and what Jesus did in the 'missing years' which we know not of. There are strong beliefs that he gained much knowledge from his travels to Egypt, India and the Middle East. Whatever the facts are, one thing is certain, Jesus had a wonderful knowledge of healing. His message was simple and direct, he preached a Gospel of love and compassion and, with a simple laying on of hands, was able to make blind men see and lame men throw away their crutches and walk.

His message to all was simple: "Spread the Gospel and heal the sick". He taught us to try to love one another, to love God and to do God's work.

He told us that all healing comes from God, the divine source, and that "God is Love". So in touch with His Father in Heaven was He that He knew when, how and where He was going to be put to death. He knew, of those closest to Him, who would betray Him, and how.

His legacy to us was for we healers to follow the principles He enunciated to heal the sick. He said, "Greater things than I have done—will you also do."

Because all healing comes from God we can be sure that this same healing energy is with us today.

His disciples went out to the world to spread the gospel of His teachings and thus the Christian Church was begun. The Roman Emperor Constantine tried to use Christianity as a way to unite the Western World under Rome. He forced thousands to accept his Religion by the use of force. From this time onwards there was a declining interest in spiritual ideas and doctrines, and the path of spiritual healing becomes harder to trace. Obviously, things were happening around the world but there seemed no clear picture of events until the Europe of the Middle Ages.

During this time we see the growth of orthodox medicines, and the growing power which the Churches were exerting. The Churches were becoming more and more powerful and would brook no opposition. During this period people who were healers, clairvoyant or had other gifts, were said to be witches and many thousands were put to death by orders of the Church. Joan of Arc, who heard a voice which told her that she would lead an army of France against the British and defeat them, was put to death because she became too popular with the people. She had the gift of clairaudience—she received messages from Spirit. Isn't it a good job we live now and not in those days gone by, otherwise we would have been burnt at the stake for our troubles.

In the Eighteenth Century the Kings and Queens of England and France were to further healing by the laying on of hands, by what was known as the 'King's Touch', and many of their subjects were said to have been cured by their touch.

Progress for spiritual healing was slow but steady and we are approaching another era in its development. We now have the birth of modern Spiritualism, a movement that was to sweep America and England. As we now know, it was Spiritualism and all that it offered which was to contribute most to the spread of spiritual healing, in that it did accept that Spirit were active in our physical world. Much valuable proof was given through the mediums of that day, and more was becoming known of how Spirit affect us in our world and of the Healing Energy that is available. We see the work of such people as Franz Mesmer and Emmanuel Swedenborg, and their theories and experiments on hypnosis and magnetic energies.

The people of that day were searching for new ideas and beliefs and Spiritualist churches and seances were springing up everywhere. It was the golden age of the Spiritual Medium (our modern day Tarot reader or clairvoyant). People with these gifts were no longer burnt at the stake. Such people as the Fox sisters, Emma Harding Britten, and Allen Kardec and many others were in the vanguard of this new movement. Spiritual healing and spirit gifts were becoming more accepted. By the 1930s onwards such Healers as

Harry Edwards, Ted Fricker and Billy Parish were doing great work and getting incredible results.

In the 1950s the Archbishop of Canterbury convened a Commission to look into spiritual healing for the Church of England. Sadly, though, the church hierarchy decided not to make it public. Was this because it found so much praise for spiritual healing, which was at this time being performed by healers outside the Churches and not by the priests? Mr Harry Edwards, the most famous healer since Jesus Christ, attempted to prove to both the Church and the British Medical Association that spiritual healing worked, and did help many people when orthodox medicine failed them. Despite the fact that he had so much documented evidence with 100% proof, he was unable to change their opinions. Sadly, we see much the same attitude by some of today's medical profession. Fortunately, we are seeing some changes here, and some medical doctors are open to the way complementary therapies work.

In 1955 Harry Edwards formed the National Federation of Spiritual Healers, a non denominational Group. This association has grown tremendously, and today is probably the foremost and most respected group for spiritual healers in the world.

As you can see spiritual healing has been with us for thousands of years and I'm sure will be with us for years to come. There does seem to be a quickening in the pace of learning and understanding. We are seeing more people turning to spiritual healing, both as healers and those seeking healing.

The source of all healing is God. God is Spirit, and as we are Spirit we can receive this healing energy as part of God's divine plan for mankind. All spiritual healing is subject to spiritual laws, and every healing is a planned act directed by an intelligence far superior to our human one. Both physical and spiritual laws combine in harmony to make the healing possible, just as there must be harmony between our spirit guides, the healer and the patient. All healing is totally controlled by Spirit, with us, the healer, being used by Spirit to transform the spirit energy into energy able to be accepted by the physical body.

I have had to make this history of healing fairly brief and to focus on some of the important points. You are of course aware that a whole book could be written on this subject.

6

Just What is Spiritual Healing?

I have thought long and hard about how I should go about explaining spiritual healing. It would be easy to trot out the usual formula in words, but I feel that there is more that should be understood about the subject, to enable us to really have an appreciation of what it is. If a person who knows nothing about the subject comes to you, they will have questions to ask. As a healer, you will be better equipped to answer them if you are able to provide some background information.

Remember not everyone is like you in his or her beliefs, although I believe that most people who go to a healer really do want to believe, and are the ones most likely to be receptive to new ideas. If you imagine yourself in your client's position, would you really be impressed if the healer seemed to be reading from a prepared card? The words of explanation should come from the heart and not from the head only.

Spiritual healing is and always should be the simplicity of gently laying on of hands. This humble act, combined with our attunement with our spirit guides, allows the spiritual energies to flow from the divine source to heal the sick; whether in body, mind or spirit.

These energies from the spiritual source are transformed from the spiritual level by the agency of a person who has the gift of healing. This energy is then able to be transferred to the patient, where it can induce a beneficial effect upon the patient's energy field.

Quite simply, the energy flows are:

From Spirit —	Through Spirit —	To Spirit
The divine	The spirit of the	The spirit of
source	healer	the patient

Spiritual healing is a spiritual act and LOVE is the force that motivates it.

I feel that there needs to be a more sincere and committed approach to spiritual healing, because Love is and has to be the main component of the healing act. We must not forget that we as healers are 'sowers of seeds', and if we can explain the process clearly, the client will be better able to relate the details to others.

It is important to encourage an open mind. Explain that spiritual healing is non-denominational; we are not Catholic healers or Protestant healers, we are 'spiritual healers'. We believe in a God and a Spirit (Soul) and also in reincarnation. We are not alone in these views, for every major religion holds very similar beliefs. There may be some variations in their interpretation but there is a lot of common ground. We are not just a physical body: we also possess a mind and a spirit.

The Spirit is the life force which motivates the physical body and as such is infinite (it never dies), whereas the physical body is finite. Death occurs when the Spirit or consciousness leaves the body to continue its development, and the body is either buried or cremated. The real you does not die but lives on in another realm as part of the soul's journey of progress towards perfection. Everything was created by God: nature, the seasons, the human body, and we must marvel at this excellence.

All healing energy and power comes from God, and when there is healing work to be done His healing ambassadors in Spirit (our guides) direct healing energy from the spirit realm to the healer (who has the gift of healing) in our material world. The healer under the direction of the healing guides, who are masters in the manipulation of spiritual energy, are able with the simple laying on of hands to bring about changes to the sick person; whether in body, mind or spirit. The spirit energy flowing into the patient's physical body is able to establish harmony where there was disharmony (disease). The flow of energy is controlled and directed by our friends in spirit using we healers in the physical world as a channel for the energy.

So now we can understand that spiritual healing is a gift from God to all we humans in this world, irrespective of colour, race or creed. It is part of a Divine Plan to promote our spiritual growth whilst we live on earth.

It must be fully understood that it is not we physical beings who do the healing. We play our part in the healing act, but it is controlled and ordered by a far higher intelligence than ours. Nothing occurs by chance. All healing is a planned act, and we place all aspects of diagnosis, direction of energy, and technique in the capable hands of our spirit guides.

The faculty of spiritual healing is divinely bestowed by Spirit. It is an ability that we as a Spirit have worked hard to develop, in our previous incarnations, to get to the stage of spiritual development which we are now at. This is why some people who are healers seem to posses far stronger healing powers than others. These healers are more developed spiritually, due to the healing work in which they have participated in previous lives. In fact they are what I would like to call 'more developed souls'. I would be quite sure in saying that you and your spirit helpers have worked together in a healing capacity in previous incarnations. I believe also that many of the people with whom you come in contact will also have worked with you in a previous life, in a healing environment. It is an example of 'Wisdom', and understanding which is born with us, and brought in from previous lives. It contrasts with 'Knowledge', which can be learned by the reading of books, or attending classes.

To illustrate my point I would draw your attention to the classical masters Beethoven and Mozart, who were composing and playing symphonies in their early childhood. We can not teach a child to produce such works; it therefore signifies that they were born with this wonderful ability. These are examples of what we today call 'genius'; they were 'gifted' individuals.

7

Bringing it All Together

I have thought a great deal about how I should write this book and what form it should take to enable people to get results from it for themselves.

I feel guided to put it together in a similar way to my Spiritual Healing Course, with a chapter covering each subject, going through from the starting point when we first meet to the end result, which will be the 'hands on' stage, when a student puts into practice what has been learnt from the beginning.

I shall at all times try to explain things to you as simply as I can, so that it will be easy for you to understand. Many books, I believe, are becoming too technical and including many things that are irrelevant for you in your quest to be a spiritual healer. Now that you have your own copy of this book you will find it very handy to keep nearby and to use as a reference as you proceed with your journey into spiritual healing.

I would first like to put it to you that you are not reading this book by accident, coincidence, or whatever you may wish to call it. I believe that you have been directed to this book by your spirit friends. It may have attracted your attention in a bookshop, been given as a present or recommended to you. It really doesn't matter, for you now have the book, and may I say this, if you don't enjoy it when you have read it, please keep quiet and say nothing. But if you did enjoy the book, tell all your friends, write to the newspapers, and broadcast it to everyone you meet! Joking, of course.

Better to ask a question than to remain ignorant forever.

As I mentioned previously I do not believe in so-called 'coincidences'. When Spirit are working with us we are somehow guided, and I'm sure you all have some personal stories to tell on the subject. Some of you will have been told by clairvoyants that you have healing ability, either by the medium seeing certain colours around you which indicate healing ability, or you may receive a message from Spirit suggesting that you try to develop your gift.

It may also be that you have had thoughts or feelings about spiritual healing before but never took it any further, until now when the time is becoming right for you to progress. You will be fulfilling your spiritual destiny, which you yourself chose before you were born into this world. So you can see by this that there are forces at work here which will play a big part in your life to come. It is starting to open up to you and as you progress then more will be given to you.

Only when the pupil is ready—does the Teacher arrive!

Spiritual healing must never be seen as a 'competition', for example, to see who is the best, or strongest healer in the Group. This can and indeed does happen with some people, particularly in the early days of development and I shall deal with this problem in the section entitled 'The Human Element'. Be aware of it and don't let it happen to you.

On every course I have facilitated I have asked the group "Is there anybody here who doesn't believe in an after-life, reincarnation or a spirit world and spirit people?" Luckily I have had no one who didn't believe. Otherwise I feel we would have had to refund their money.

We must have a faith and belief in the Spirit world for how could we possibly strive to become spiritual healers? It does all come back to having a personal faith and belief in our spirit friends, for we are really dealing with something we cannot prove. One lady told me that she could prove it because she had seen her Grandmother at the foot of her bed the night before. How wonderful and uplifting for her, but this could not be used in the general manner of things as proof (to the public): sceptics could say she was dreaming or hallucinating etc.

Truly it does come back to our own personal beliefs, and more people are coming to accept these beliefs in today's changing world. In times gone by I am sure many of you who may have seen or heard something would not have been able to tell anybody, even a close friend or relative, for fear they may have thought that you had 'lost the plot'. Now, thank goodness, this is changing for the better.

You can do very little with faith—but you can do nothing without it.

8

The Therapy of the Future

It is evident that more and more people are now becoming interested in learning about spiritual ideas and concepts. I believe this to be part of the 'Big Plan' that Spirit tell us about. Do you not feel that changes are happening all around us? In the past, media such as the newspapers, television, etc., somehow seemed to try to ridicule programs that were about psychic or spiritual matters. It may only have been an adverse comment but it was there. How things have changed: more and more people are interested in such subjects, and the Media treat them with a lot more respect. In Perth, Western Australia we took a big step forward when I was able to have spiritual healing accepted as a recognised course for the Technical and Further Education Department of the West Australian Government. Establishing credibility was a primary factor, which played a major role in TAFE's decision to include spiritual healing amongst its courses. My membership of the National Federation of Spiritual Healers (UK) and the fact that their code of conduct was drawn up in conjunction with the British Medical Association convinced the directors that spiritual healing was a credible healing art. Slowly and surely things are moving forward, and so we as spiritual healers must take heart, have patience, and endeavour to play our part in the 'Big Plan'.

For all of we healers who wish to devote our time to the cause, let us always remember that:

Service to our fellow human beings and animals is the way forward.

I can put it in no simpler terms than to say that we who practise spiritual healing, and in fact any person who lives their life in a spiritual way, are all 'Sowers of Seeds'.

By our ideals and the way we live our life, trying to be of service to others, we hope that who so ever we meet along the path may also try to offer the hand of friendship to those in need, that they meet on their journey through life.

In the words of that Master healer, Jesus Christ, "Spread the word and heal the sick."

My wish in writing this book is to reveal how spiritual healing, performed by those humans who are endowed with this gift, can be used by our friends in the spirit realm to heal the sick, be they ill in body, mind or spirit. This will lead to a better, more peaceful, and more spiritual way of life in the future. Spirit will do their part to make the necessary changes; let us ensure that we in turn will be doing ours.

As a spiritual healer working for Spirit in the physical world, I feel impelled to make this comparison: we as healers are akin to the scalpel in the hands of an accomplished surgeon in the operating theatre.

9

What did the Early Philosophers say about Spirit?

As spiritual healers it is quite likely that you will be asked questions about our spirit (soul) and I'm sure there will be many you feel you cannot answer. Please do not let this worry you for there are many aspects of the Spirit we are unable to explain, for they are beyond our human comprehension. The question of whether the spirit is in the body or the body in the spirit cannot be answered. As spirit and physical body are connected in a divine way by spiritual means, no limitations could be placed on Spirit. There are many things to do with healing that we do not need to be able to prove or understand; let us trust in Spirit and leave all in their capable hands.

I am sure we all have our own opinions on the subject and it has proved very handy to me when discussing spirit and spiritual healing to be able to offer some of the beliefs of very learned philosophers of earlier times.

We do not know when or why men and women first began to ask questions on whether we are more than a physical body. All of us want to know what happens to us when we meet physical death. Looking at it logically, if we do go to another place (call it Heaven if you wish) then it must also be true to say that we lived a life before this one. There are so many question and so few answers. So let us look at what the early Philosophers said about the subject and whilst they may vary slightly in their definitions, they do basically agree on the subject.

In the 6th century Greece, a teacher and philosopher called Anaximenes stated that the soul of man was very much like air, in that it could not actually be seen or touched. Like the air about us, which holds together all things in the Universe, so too did the soul (spirit) hold together the human body.

Another Greek philosopher, Empedocles, argued that men do not only live in this physical world, they have another existence which goes far beyond the purely material. There is a part of man which is eternal.

To Plato, the soul was indestructible: it always exists. The spirit exists in some other realm until for whatever reason it takes on a physical body, and once that function in the physical world has been fulfilled, it progresses into the spiritual realm. The soul was also indestructible and was infinite whereas the physical body is finite.

Aristotle believed that every form of life had a soul, but the soul of mankind was far more sophisticated and was endowed with powers beyond that of animals.

St. Augustine felt that humans consisted of a spirit (soul) and a physical body, which made a union for the life on earth. When the union has completed its function and there is a parting, it is then that the Soul goes to its perfect state in another realm.

Albert the Great, a physician of the Roman Catholic Church, believed the soul to be immortal, and saw the body as simply an extension of the soul. The body was necessary to the soul in the material world only inasmuch as it gave the soul another dimension and awareness.

The Spanish Philosopher Juan Luis Vives saw the soul of man as the driving force, the animation, which motivated the physical body. He also felt that any attempts to understand how the spirit functions are beyond the comprehension of mankind.

John Locke believed that the universe consisted of two basic elements, a spiritual one and a physical one. The spirit (soul) was immaterial but did possess an intelligence, and interacted with the physical body. He saw the soul as the driving force behind the physical body and with this interaction the experiences thus gained enabled the spirit to progress.

The ideas that have been given may be of help to you should you ever be asked for some opinions on survival after death.

Many things cannot be proved, and many things we cannot understand. Please don't get too concerned about this: I do not believe it is too important for you to be an expert.

Think about this: When you get into your car to drive off somewhere, do you have to know exactly how the engine and gearbox, etc. work? Of course you don't.

When you switch the light on in your lounge room, do you know, or can you explain how the bulb lights up, or how it all works? Again, of course not.

When you switch on your television set, how many of us understand how it works, and how the picture appears on the screen? The details of how these things happen, we don't need to know.

I have asked my guide if he could explain to me how spiritual healing works. His answer was: "Of course I can explain it to you but you would not understand, for it is beyond your comprehension".

We must have faith and trust in our spirit friends.

10

Use of the Word 'Spirit' in Everyday Life

To people with an open mind the word spirit is quite acceptable, for we know that we are a spirit which takes on a physical body for its earthly experience. Some people, however, cannot accept 'spirit' or 'spiritual' as anything other than conjuring up a vision of people in orange robes and bald heads, chanting and banging tambourines in the street. Nothing is further from the truth and as more and more people are awakening to the spiritual, we shall see a big change in attitudes.

The word spirit or spiritual is used many times in our everyday life by people who, whilst they may not believe, nevertheless use the word.

Some examples:

Free spirit	Holy Spirit	Low spirits	High spirits	Good spirits
Bad spirits	Fighting spirit	Broken spirit	Kindred spirits	Spirit guides
Need to raise their spirits	Plenty of spirit	He or she is very spiritual	Spiritualism as a religion	Spiritual healing
The spirit is willing but the flesh is weak.				

These are but a few examples which are common in daily life. Another could be at a football match, where one supporter is heard to say about his team, "They need more fighting spirit".

When asked about what is meant by the word 'spiritual', or leading a more 'spiritual life', many people say things like: "I go to church and pray every Sunday"; or "I say my prayers every night to God". This they may do, but they still continue doing other things like being selfish, greedy, doing things for themselves to the detriment of others; in some instances, lying, cheating for their own ends. Some people say, "Well, I meditate every day," or "I keep to myself and don't bother anyone". I'm sure you have heard many things like this.

We live in probably the most materialistic period in history— money is the god to be worshipped. Even human life itself is not valued as much as money. We see this in the tragedies all over the world: people starving in Africa, thousands dying—once we turn off the TV, we soon forget about it. Most people worship the almighty dollar, have everything they need and more, and yet are not happy and never will be, because money and what it will buy will not bring happiness.

We need to get back to our spiritual roots to truly achieve that inner peace and happiness. Put very simply 'spiritual' only means 'service': helping our fellow man, when they are in times of need: a comforting word, an arm around the shoulder, a listening ear, a hand stretched out in friendship unconditionally.

As you develop and progress more into spiritual healing you will be rewarded more than you can know by the smile on the face, and the "thank you" from a person helped by that Spirit energy which has flowed through you to that person; for we know that what we have done has come from the heart—with love. For love is the strongest force in the universe.

We are humans living in a material, mercenary world with all its problems and disasters and we will undoubtedly fail and make mistakes, but if we try to be of service to others and we do it from love, then our loving friends in Spirit will be with us to guide and help us, giving us their love, the feeling and receiving of which is overwhelming.

The spiritual path is not an easy one; it would be of no value if it were; but there is a purpose and a meaning behind it all, and with the help of our spirit friends we shall make it, for they will help us up when we fall and whilst they will not 'do it for us', we only need ask and we shall be given, for they love us with a love beyond our understanding.

11

The Scientist's View of Spirit

We humans see life in the physical form, and as being three-dimensional. As we go through life we gain experience through the five physical senses we possess; namely sight, smell, touch, taste and hearing, and we have developed these senses to a very high state.

One could say that we have progressed faster in the last fifty years than we did in the previous five hundred. Our scientists have developed some wonderful technology, especially in communications, transport, flight, computers and many more too numerous and diversified to discuss. Yes! We have done wonders, but sadly it hasn't all been for the benefit of mankind. We can deliver weapons of war quicker, computers have made many people lose their jobs. Some people and companies have gained enormous wealth. All this technology has only served to make us chase affluence, and made us very materialistic in our lives. Of course, there have been good outcomes and we are thankful for them. In chasing affluence, we have totally ignored the fundamental questions appertaining to people's spiritual and mental health. Their state of mind, matters of the heart and the soul, and their attitudes, are all totally ignored and their emotions and feelings forgotten.

Scientists believe they can explain everything by scientific means, but one cannot solve spiritual questions with scientific answers. As science has progressed, many scientists are discovering that not everything can be explained in the physical.

Nobel Prize winning scientist John Eccles wrote that science cannot explain the creation of each of us as individuals; nor can scientists answer such fundamental questions as, 'Who am I? Why am I here? What happens after death?' These are all mysteries, which are beyond a scientific explanation.

And of course scientists, being what they are, would want to contact it and find out more about it. Some people with scientific backgrounds have been instrumental in spreading spiritualism and contact with the spirit world, among them such well known figures as Sir Arthur Conan-Doyle, the creator of the Sherlock Holmes, Sir William Crookes, the renowned English physicist and Air Chief Marshall Lord Dowding of 2nd World War fame.

The inventor Thomas Edison was working on an electronic machine with which he hoped to establish communication with Spirit. Much research is being done in the field of 'electronic voice phenomena' using tape recorders and voices said to be of deceased people such as Winston Churchill, Napoleon and Jesus Christ have allegedly been recorded.

Who knows, maybe in the future our scientific friends may make a breakthrough. For myself, I feel it will only be if Spirit so desires it, but if scientists can adopt a more spiritual approach to their work it must surely be good for mankind.

12

Belief in a God in the Major World Religions

As we can see, all the major religions in this world have a belief in a God; they may differ somewhat in their interpretations but all have basically the same beliefs.

So as you can see, when we say we believe in God, we are not alone; millions of people believe the same as we do. Belief in God or whatever name you wish to put to God, is your personal choice. It may be the Great Spirit, Universal Energy, The Absolute or whatever you feel comfortable with.

	CHRISTIANITY	HINDUISM	ISLAM	JUDAISM	SHINTOISM
God as the Highest Power	God the Almighty Seeing God as male form	Brahman, the Soul of the Universe, Seeing God as neither male or female.	Allah, which means God Seeing God as male form.	The Jews speak of God as male form	Spirit is in all Nature
GOD as the Supreme	God as the Father	Shiva, Vishnu Brahma	Allah is all powerful	God gave His people the 10 Commandments	Until the end of the 2nd World War the Emperor was like God
GOD as Inspirator	God as the Holy Spirit	Shakti	Allah revealed all to Muhammad	The Jews believe that they are God's Chosen People	There are Male and Female Spirits

GOD in Human Form	Jesus Christ as Son of God	The Soul is in all living things.	The Muslims revere Allah	There are none but the one God	The Spirit is Divine
GOD Reaching Divinity	The various Saints or Angels	Hindu Gods can take on human form Sai-Baba	There is only one God. All else is forbidden	There are none but the one God	The Spirits of deceased persons are revered
GOD'S Messengers	The Prophets	Guru's, Wise men ie. Sai-Baba Krishnamurti	Muhammad, who became a teacher	The Elders ie. Abraham and Moses	Revered Spirits
Belief in Reincarnation	Resurrection of Jesus Christ	A belief that the Spirit goes on after physical death	Belief in Allah and the teachings ensures life after death	In doing the Will of God, they will become one with God	Belief in the path of the Spirit through many lives

These details I have presented are only meant to be a guide for you and are not an in-depth analysis. I realise that more wars are fought over religious beliefs than many other things and I don't want to end up being another Salman Rushdie.

13

Reincarnation and the Spirit (Soul)

Reincarnation is a word derived from Latin, used by occultists to mean the repeated descent of the human spirit from the spiritual realm into the physical body. Almost all doctrines teach that the purpose of reincarnation is the evolution and expansion of the spirit through experiences that can only be gained on this earthly plane. We could say that the earth life for us is a school, a place we come to learn and experience every aspect that we need to overcome, in order to progress towards becoming a more complete (spiritual) person. It is said that if we don't learn our lesson in this life we shall come back again and have another go. We cannot 'buck the system'; the laws are perfect; it seems we shall all have to try harder.

If we look at the subject logically we can only determine that if reincarnation was not a fact, and that if this was the one and only life we would have, don't you think it would be a pointless exercise, a sick joke? It wouldn't make sense, would it? There would be no reason or purpose behind our life. Think about it! Our spirit friends talk much of the 'law of cause and effect'; in other words, *As you sow, so shall you reap.*

Whatever deeds one does, be they good or bad, we shall have to answer for them. We cannot escape, all is known.

I can picture someone arriving in the spirit world and being asked by the Almighty, "What about that situation when you ran off with the money for the orphans' Christmas party?"

"But, but nobody found out about me doing that: I wasn't caught."

And the answer booming out loudly, "But I knew!"

I do believe that Spirit do know everything we do; all is noted, and as I have been told, they see what is in our hearts. We may convince others and ourselves but 'they know'.

All major Religions express a belief in reincarnation, though they may differ in their expressions on the subject.

RELIGIOUS DOCTRINE	THE ORIGIN OF THE SOUL	THE PATH OF THE SOUL	THE DESTINY OF THE SOUL
CHRISTIANITY	A Spirit created by God inhabits each new body	The Soul and the physical body separate at death	That there will be a Resurrection in some form on the day of Judgement
JUDAISM	The same belief basically as the Christians	The Spirit leaves and goes back to God	That there will be a day of Judgement and a Resurrection
BUDDHISM	Part of the Universal Soul resides for a period of time on earth in a physical body	On physical death the Soul, after a time, moves to another physical body	The Spirit goes to find paradise with God
HINDUISM	The Spirit begins in the animal kingdom and then progresses to a human incarnation	The Spirit leaves the body and after a period of time takes on another body according to its stage of evolution	In the end the Spirit goes to God and has no more incarnations
TAOISM	The spirit (soul) has two parts, yang, which is the Spiritual part and yin which is the physical part	At physical death the spirit (yang) leaves the body and goes to God, the yin (earthly body) returns to the earth and is no more	The soul (spirit) returns to God and becomes a controlling spirit for its ancestors to help those on earth

The above chart is really put forward as a guide for you, as to the Spirit and other religions, to help you should you be asked by one of your patients during a conversation. Like all religious arguments and opinions, there is no one answer that is always right; don't forget we all have our opinions—let others have theirs.

As one door closes, another opens.

14

Searching and Finding

I have been told many times over the last 10 years or so by Spirit communications that I would write a book. I wasn't told what sort of book, and frankly I had no interest whatsoever in doing such a thing. I do not know how to write, print, publish and distribute a book. I have finally accomplished this huge task and hope that this book will be well received and of use to many people.

By nature I am quite sceptical, my birth sign is Virgo with Virgo rising, so as you can see this would tend to give me a preference for things I can prove. I would hasten to say that I do have an open mind and I am very open to new ideas. In my early years I must admit that I did live life to the full and enjoyed the pleasures of the very materialistic society we live in, and because of this I was very reluctant in my approach to, and getting involved in, spiritual healing. It was as if I were being manoeuvred by something; some power was directing me. People would comment that they couldn't see me being involved in spiritual healing, as I was so down to earth, and very practical and logical in my approach to things.

Once I became involved I determined that if I was going to be a healer, I wanted to be a genuine Healer, a good one. The credibility of healing has always been of paramount importance to me, because it's the only way for spiritual healing to progress. It was when I read books by Harry Edwards, Maurice Tester and Ted Fricker that I could see that my ideas were going in the right direction. These healers taught that spiritual healing was very simply and basically performed, exactly the same way that the master healer Jesus Christ healed. A very simple 'laying on of hands' is all that is needed. These wonderful healers knew that it wasn't them that were responsible for the miracles that happened and they said so. Our spirit friends, guides, doctors, whatever you may call them, working under God's direction, are the ones doing the healing. These healers, mentioned earlier, played their part in the healing act but trusted, and had utmost belief in, their spirit friends.

- Keep trusting Spirit, they are guiding you well.
- It is they who control every aspect of healing.
- Simple laying on of hands is the way to go.
- Sincere motives, from the heart, are the only thoughts required.

The more I am involved in spiritual healing, the more I become aware of the fact that it is Spirit who control every aspect and detail of the healing. We play our part in the healing act and even though it is only a small part it is nevertheless a really important part. We are working with Spirit in a joint effort, under their guidance.

I would say this to you: *You don't choose them—they choose you!*

Whatever healing ability you have was divinely bestowed by God before you were born into this world; your life was charted, your gift there to be used to help mankind, and your free will was offered also, so that you had a choice in this lifetime.

All is known about you by Spirit, your state of spiritual development, and the strength of your gift, your character and nature. The reason that Spirit gives you a test is quite simply to test your desire to heal, for it is your choice, isn't it? Free will plays its part here. Will you complete your destiny or will you succumb to the earthly desires and pleasures?

We are in what people call 'the new age'; it's new age thinking they say. Is it really? Isn't it more likely to be to some people the New Age of making money, and making it quick? Think about it; we are dealing with things we cannot prove, and so it is quite easy for any of us to be deceived by dishonest people. I think that in most people there is a part of us that 'wants to believe', and this is why we can so often be deceived.

Let me say this: "Of course there are many genuine people out there, doing their best and doing a wonderful job." But there are also many who are doing their best to get your money into their hot little hands.

How does this come about? Well, we are all searching, and in many cases very vulnerable. We want to believe, and when we want to believe we can easily accept what someone tells us. We have seen an incredible increase in the amount of clairvoyants and tarot card readers, psychic artists, rebirthers, regressionists, and all manner of others who have thought up some fantastic names for their therapies, many of which I fear have little substance, and few of their practitioners have genuine qualifications. It never ceases to amaze me what some people will do to make a quick buck. Take a look at some of the courses being offered out there, and they are not cheap either, all seemingly there to make you an instant expert in several easy lessons. There are so many courses and workshops on offer, covering a multitude of subjects, that one needs to do some research to make sure that it is what you feel you want to do. Trust your own intuition.

I believe a healer is born with the 'gift of healing'; it is a gift of the Spirit, and whilst we can all heal to a degree, I believe that it is only those gifted ones who are spiritually developed who will develop their wonderful gift to its fullest potential. You cannot take people off the street and make them into healers, as Spirit says!

If you are not ready to receive it, you cannot obtain it.

At a very early age Beethoven was composing and playing symphonies. No, you cannot teach anyone to do that—he was born with the gift. But hey, don't get downhearted—I'm sure we all have to go through many trials and tribulations to achieve our goal. Use your intuition, your inner feelings; search around, try different people and groups until you find where you feel comfortable. If you find somewhere and it doesn't feel comfortable, then it is not for you! Yes! Be sceptical; cross-reference everything, and check if the same things keep coming up. You will be guided to where is best for you.

As they say, "You have to kiss a lot of frogs, before you find a Prince." Follow your inner feelings. You will only know a genuine one when you have met some insincere ones.

15

Universal Laws—Putting Balance in our Lives

As we journey through life we shall experience many things. It could be said that some are good and some are bad. It is necessary for us to have these experiences as they are vital to our development.

To help us to put into perspective some of the experiences we may have during our life we need to understand the universal laws.

LAW OF OPPOSITES

Highs and lows: We must have depressions and low periods in our lives so that we can appreciate the highs.

Good and Bad: We need to experience bad things so that we can fully experience the good things in our lives. For example, a bad relationship makes you appreciate a good relationship.

We need both for us to have more understanding.

There has to be positive and negative in our lives to enable us to be able to appreciate what a wonderful world we live in. Try to think positively all the time.

LAW OF ACTION

Anything we do will be added to. If we do nothing then nothing happens—we must start to do something. If you are feeling depressed then put action into operation, go for a walk, clean the car.

Remember: *The journey of a thousand miles begins with the first step.*

So when you are feeling down, and seemingly lacking energy or direction, get out into nature, breathe the air, look at the flowers.

LAW OF LEVITATION

What goes up must come down—our feelings go up and down, our moods fluctuate, we need this. Nobody can be up all the time—we are all human. Remember: when you are feeling really down that there is only one way, and that is up.

LAW OF CAUSE AND EFFECT

With every action (cause) there is a re-action (effect). Everything we say or do has an effect, something happens. As we sow—so we shall reap. As we give so we receive. What goes around comes around. Be it in this life or the next one. Nothing is missed.

If only all people on earth could follow this ideal, how much better could life be. If people knew that they would answer for their crimes, I'm sure they wouldn't do them.

LAW OF DELIVERANCE

Everything has a start and a finish. We are born into this world, with a plan to achieve. We play our part on the stage of life, learning and doing, until we have played our part to the best we can fulfil. Physical death comes and the spirit goes on to another realm, to maybe repeat the lessons, until finally we reach God.

THE LAW OF KARMA

Our life has a plan to it. There is a reason for everything—nothing is by chance. All is perfect: out of something which may appear to us as bad, will come something good. We will all answer for our actions, good or bad.

These are some of the basic aids for us to live by and to take into perspective when we journey on our path through life. The main point, which comes from this, is that we do need a balance in our lives. If we look at nature we see a perfect, balanced system operating—a perfect system, in which every plant, animal, fish, etc., plays its part. The seasons, the tides, the sun rising and setting, all is balanced. Just imagine if there were to be a change in the seasons—we would see chaos. If we took the bees and butterflies out of the system—then no flowers, fruit trees etc. would be pollinated—so no food supply—again chaos.

If we don't have balance in our lives we shall eventually cause sickness in our bodies, for we have disharmony.

- If we work too much and sleep too little.
- If we drink too much and don't eat properly.
- If we worry about material things and neglect the Spiritual.

Of course there are many other examples of imbalance which will lead to sickness.

Because we humans are not just a physical body, but are also mind and spirit we must endeavour to keep a balance between these three parts and in doing so we shall start to see a happier more contented life and this will be of great benefit to us. So be aware that we do, all of us, need to have negative and positive in our lives, just keep that balance: everything in moderation.

Moderation is essential in all things.

16

The Way Forward

I believe that for spiritual healing to become more recognised and accepted by both the medical profession and the general public we must be seen to be both credible and genuine in all that we do. As spiritual healing becomes more popular we shall see some people attracted to it who do not have the right motives, and such is the nature of spiritual healing that these people can be quite hard to spot. Looking at this situation in a logical and factual way we accept that all professions, be they medical, legal or otherwise, have their quota of dubious practitioners, and make no mistake, we in the Healing Profession also have our share of dodgy therapists. It never ceases to amaze me as to what lengths some humans will go to make a dollar. It seems that their idea is to make it sound very mystical and mysterious and to charge accordingly. We now see aura cleaners, chakra balancers, openers and closers, and human being healers who profess to be healing the etheric body. What used to be called simply a 'massage' becomes a 'psychodynamic therapy'. I'm sure that Spirit don't want all this hype and would like us to get back to 'the old fashioned spirituality'. But let's not dwell on it; what can we do to help the growth of spiritual healing?

I would like to offer some advice, some ideas which I feel could be of help to you in assisting your progress.

Firstly, I say again that I do not believe it is by chance that you are showing interest in spiritual healing. I do believe that there is a plan behind it all which, whilst you do not see it at the present moment, will in time become more apparent to you.

I would recommend that you begin by reading books on healing. There are a lot of books on the market and I don't feel it would be right for me to recommend any. The main reason being that we are all different, and what may appeal to one person does not appeal to another. The other point to bear in mind is that each book will differ in its ideas, and so you, the reader, must choose what appeals to you. If you feel comfortable with what the book says and it sort of fits together with what you believe then try it. If what the book advises does not feel comfortable for you—then reject it and try another.

I would suggest that you make inquiries about spiritual healing groups in your area; if you know of a spiritual healer you could ask them about groups in your area. Go along and check them out see how you feel about them. If you feel comfortable and relaxed and it appeals to your inner intuition, this may be the group to join. If it doesn't for any reason feel good for you, that's your inner intuition advising you, so keep looking until you find where you feel you want to be.

I believe it is imperative for any person interested in spiritual healing to receive the right training, and a good teacher is very necessary. I would say that any good, credible group would have a course for healers to develop their ability. In my opinion, the most credible and professionally run Association for healers is the English group The National Federation of Spiritual Healers (UK).

This group has affiliates world wide, so it is quite likely that your group would have a tie-up in some way. They do have contacts in Australia, Canada, USA, Africa, Europe, etc. So even if you wrote to them for further information I'm sure they would be only too happy to help.

Remember: A conversation with a wise man is better than the reading of 100 books.

As we go into the future it is of utmost importance that we as healers do become better trained and more professional in the whole way that we approach spiritual healing. We need to work with the medical profession and not see ourselves as opposition. We must approach the doctors as a complementary therapy and definitely not as an alternative therapy. The word alternative is threatening and confrontational to the medical profession and we healers know that we can work exceptionally well in conjunction with the medical doctors. In the United Kingdom at the present moment some healers are working with GPs in surgeries. The way ahead must surely be for both groups to work together to help the sick of this world.

17

Energy: Natural/Universal

In the material world in which we live we are quite used to the word 'energy'. To us it is a symbol of power; we could say that the motor cars, factories, industry, our own homes are run by energy/power. Scientists tell us that "Energy can change from one form to another, and that it is indestructible."

To explain 'God', is beyond our comprehension. God—the Creator of all things—has been referred to as an infinite, all-powerful energy and that God is in all things, living and non-living. Again our Scientist tells us that the very chair and table we sit at, even our own physical body is not solid, it is atoms (energy) vibrating—so God is in all things.

But let's not get too technical—let's try to bring things to a level which we can understand. I believe it is very important that we as healers, when spreading the word, put things into layman's terms, for after all we are not explaining healing energies to scientists, but to ordinary people who do want to understand and learn.

Electricity exits naturally—watch a storm, see the lightning, hear the thunder. When lightning strikes it can kill, cause fires; it is a very powerful force and can be very destructive, as it cannot be controlled.

Electricity occurs everywhere, but unless we are able to convert it, control it and concentrate it through a transformer we cannot use it to flow through the wires to light the lamp or to heat the stove. So you can see that because electricity (lightning strike) is so powerful that, to be able to be used, it has to be controlled. We human beings have been able to harness electricity for the good of mankind.

Spirit energy also is everywhere, but must be controlled and concentrated through an outlet for it to be of help to those in need.

Spirit energy (healing energy) has to find a medium (physical); a wire to flow through to be used in this physical world.

Because matters of the Spirit are beyond our comprehension, we must conclude that it is a Spirit mind, which alone can control this energy. Emanating from its spiritual source, our spirit guides, or 'doctors in spirit', use this energy to help human kind in this physical world by using an outlet which is physical (human).

This is where you as a healer come in; you have the gift of Healing, which is Divinely bestowed by Spirit. And so, when God chooses to make His presence felt and to work in the material world, He does so by using a human being as His channel.

Spirit alone can control and direct Spirit energy to be used to make well the sick and troubled in our Society. Understand that it is not possible for any human being to direct this energy, although many purport to do so for a fee. Spirit alone are in control, it is not us that do the healing—we are but their channel.

18

Physical and Spiritual Energy

The physical human being can control or order physical activities, such as walking, running and jumping, all appertaining to the physical body; he has control over the physical.

The spirit guides are able to control or order any activities to do with the spirit. If Spirit wish to communicate with us in this physical world they do. If they don't wish to communicate then we are powerless to make it happen.

Therefore it must imply that universal, cosmic spiritual energy—call it what you like—can only be controlled or ordered by spirit controllers (Spirit).

A physical human being cannot control spirit energy.

If this energy (spiritual, universal) is all around us, and available to mankind, then how come it hasn't been collected, bottled or harnessed by our multinational companies, and sold for profit, which is what would happen if they could do this.

It cannot, of course, because spiritual energy, which emanates from its Divine Source, God, can only be directed or controlled by a universal or spiritual source.

By our spirit helpers—who seek to serve.

19

Technology and Life

Technology has helped us enormously; we have advanced as a civilisation more in the last fifty years than in the preceding 500.

For sure, we have had some wonderful inventions and we can put a man on the moon; we have aeroplanes that can safely carry hundreds of people and we can beam television programs around the globe. But what has this material technology also given us?

It has given us greed: people are obsessed with but a single goal: affluence or the pursuit of material things. Their lives are run by this; there is envy, jealousy and pursuit of wealth all around us. In fact we could say that money is worshipped and thus more important than human life.

Of course we know we must have progress and that the introduction of computers and robots, etc., has helped us on a material level and things can be done more quickly and more efficiently. But in the pursuit of efficiency many people only look at the profit side of the equation. What happens to the staff laid off in these instances? Who cares about their plight, their feelings, etc.? Would it not be wonderful if technology could also be used more to help our spiritual technology. For remember, and if you don't, you forget at your peril, we cannot take our wealth with us when we leave this mortal coil; for as Shakespeare aptly puts it "All the world's a stage, and we are but players". We enter from stage left, we play our part and we then depart from stage right. In other words, we come into this world with nothing material, we play our part and we then depart with nothing material!

And never forget also, "As you sow—so you shall also reap." Be it in this life or the next, for we are all of us 'Spirit', with a physical body, and when the life force leaves the body it crumbles into dust and the spirit, which is immortal, goes on to another place to be assessed in our doings on earth. No one can escape this for we are Spirit and our destiny is in the spirit realm where we will, I'm sure, meet our Maker.

Think about it and try to do some good deeds whilst you are in this particular play and before you depart it.

The time for reassessment is now!

20

What Attributes are Required to be a Healer?

During the time I have been facilitating courses on spiritual healing one of the questions that has been asked more than any other is appertaining to what abilities or qualities that person needs to become a good healer. It is of course a very valid point; we should all be made aware of what could be required of us. I started off with a small list of attributes, which I felt would be helpful to persons wishing to do the work. I think that each course I have done has brought more suggestions to the fore. I am going to set out some of these attributes, but I don't want you to panic when you read the list and say, "My goodness, I shall never be able to live up to that lot". Please don't forget we are not perfect, we are all of us humans, and we are all learning and making mistakes. We are trying to develop and to progress. Bear in mind that if we were perfect we wouldn't be here, would we!

The list I have drawn up is only meant as a guideline for you to aim for, and definitely NOT meant as some sort of pre-requisite to become a healer. If it was, then it's probable that at some time or other we should all fail. What do you think?

I am sure many of you do most of the things listed without being aware of them. Tick them off.

The Gift of Healing. A gift divinely bestowed which gives one an inner urge to help our fellow man.

The Desire to Heal. We shall have an inner desire to use our gift (it doesn't go away).

A Balanced Life. We need to have moderation in all things, smoking, drinking, etc. More positive than negative feelings.

To Have Humility. We must appreciate the great gift we have, use it wisely, try to be more humble and less egotistical.

Empathy and Compassion to Others. As Healers you will I'm sure have gone through many tough times, your life may not have been easy.

Ability to Listen and Not to Judge. Be Non-Judgemental, do not give your advice. Listen to what people say without commenting.

Detachment. One must be detached from the person's problems and definitely not take them on board. That's not to say one cannot have empathy however.

Motives. Have the right motives. Do we really want to help others or is it the money or our ego, desiring it?

Commitment. We must make a commitment, devote time, and be reliable. Don't make false promises.

Persistence. To be able to carry on when things get rough, not to lose faith if it doesn't seem to be happening. Have faith.

Love. We seek an unconditional love, a love for our fellow human beings.

A Confident Happy Disposition. Have a smile on your face, be positive, confident and happy. Your Patients will appreciate it. Be positive.

Sense of Humour. A good sense of humour is an asset. It can lighten up the situation. Be friendly.

Many of you will have ticked off most of these ideas and have probably thought up more attributes. Good on you!

Don't forget to keep your healing Simple and Sincere.

By becoming more involved in spiritual healing you will be following your destiny—the plan for your life.

God enters by a private door into every individual.

21

The Creative Mind—
Negative and Positive

The mind can be very creative or very destructive and the thoughts that emanate from our minds are generally described as 'negative' or 'positive', and can most definitely influence our health. The experts tell us that we only use 5-8% of our brain and so we are left wondering what the other 95% is doing.

The mind is an incredibly powerful force and the thoughts that are received and sent by it are equally as strong. Thoughts are real forces; we have the power to either accept or dismiss a thought, and to insert a thought into our minds at any time.

The way we think, our attitudes, habits and beliefs form the basis of our success or failure.

As humans we are not so much worried or disturbed by our situation, as by our thoughts, the way we think about things, how we feel about them; then our emotions make it into reality.

When we look at the material level we can say that every new invention, scientific breakthrough and technological advance began with a thought. Whilst we can say that these advances have created much positivity, we can also see that there has been much on the negative side which has also been created. So we must be aware of the balance that is required in our everyday lives. In nature we see this to perfection. Fundamental to healthy, balanced thinking is the knowledge and belief that we are a spiritual being, travelling a spiritual path through life and learning from every incident that occurs on that journey.

We should attempt to have harmony in our lives.

If you ask most people what they most want I believe most would say, "To Be Happy". Naturally some would desire money, power or some other 'ego-pleaser'; but most would want happiness, and we as spiritual people know that the happiness and peace we seek can only come from within, it cannot come from without.

22

Change of Attitude is the Key to Changing your Life and Health

When we can look at our life and see something good coming out of what we looked upon as a really bad situation. When we can also see that if we had only good happenings and no bad ones then we would not be learning anything. I call this progress.

We all have the power, the capability, to do many things; the free will to decide what we want to do. We can seek a more Spiritual Path or a more material one; to give or to take, to be negative or positive.

CONTRASTS

Positive (Good)		Negative (Bad)
Constructive	or	Destructive
Encourage	or	Discourage
Kind and Gentle	or	Cruel and Brutal
Courage	or	Cowardice
Faith	or	Mistrust
Integrity	or	Dishonesty
Light	or	Darkness
Be Cheerful	or	Despair
Give	or	Take
Love	or	Hate

Let us as healers strive to be and act as positively as we can, so that we can help to uplift those people who come to us with their negativity and so help them to convert their negative thoughts into positive thoughts which will then help them to be healed, utilising the power of their mind.

Many of the people who come to you for healing may well be at the point of time in their life when they are ready to make changes for the better. The very fact that they have met you, a healer, may be the stimulus that they need to bring about the changes. I believe that when people are ready they are guided to you.

23

Love

When we think of the human race we naturally think of the physical body, for this is what we can see. As we begin to understand more about our spiritual heritage and destiny, the evidence collected suggests that it is our soul-spirit which is our primary body, for our thoughts, feelings, will, etc., and that the physical body is only secondary.

The physical body is the vehicle which the spirit uses for its sojourn on earth and when this period ends, the physical body is released and the spirit departs to the next stage of its development.

As souls or spirits we are always in touch with the spirit world, even though you may not be aware of this. Your spiritual faculties may be clouded and your sensitiveness dulled by mental activity and desires such as greed, envy, jealousy, etc., so that no conscious intercourse can take place, even though the spirit world is all around us and our spirit friends so close.

The foundation for all spiritual growth is 'love'. All Spirit teachings are based on love. We all like to love and to be loved, it is natural and makes us feel uplifted and improves our lives in many ways. Most of us simply do not understand love, or are unable to put it into words. It is usually used in the same context as sex. In fact, we could say that love is the most misused word in our language.

Love has many aspects and each type of love that we experience is helping us to reach that understanding of what is meant by Perfect Love. It will take the spirit many incarnations to come to appreciate love in its purest form. For we humans on earth, love is understanding our emotions and being able to forgive those who do wrong by us. Be aware that love may not be all sweetness and joy; we will experience all sorts of other emotions like anger, sorrow, jealousy, etc. We will hurt and in turn be hurt. We will contain and we will release.

If we are able to understand why a person has wronged us, we are able to forgive with love. We then have learned a valuable lesson, which is to be in control of our emotions and of the situation. Love is a powerful force for good and love is the catalyst for all healing which takes place.

The love that comes to us from Spirit, because it is so freely and lovingly given, surpasses what we humans know as love. It will only be when we have experienced this spiritual love that we can truly come to understand the full emotions that real love can bring to us.

Real love (spiritual love): Loves the other person for themselves. It asks nothing in return and is given freely. Love can be neither bought nor sold. Its only price is love.

Unreal or sentimental love: Enjoys the feelings, which the other person arouses or stimulates. The feeling or emotion called love is centred upon one person.

It is nigh on an impossible task for us to know the true meaning of spiritual love, for we must seek to find that divine love for all people.

True spiritual love is unconditional. Love is never wasted; even if it has no effect on the receiver, it benefits the giver.

As healers we know that the majority of the people who come to us suffer what I shall call mental illness, and I don't mean that they are mad. They are suffering emotional, mental (mind) problems which stress people out, and which will, if not treated, then lead to a physical problem. For example, a person who worries a great deal could end up with an ulcer. It is my belief that spiritual healing is an ideal therapy for the coming era, when I believe we shall see much more of these psychosomatic illnesses occurring. So let us look positively towards the Future.

Love conquers all things.

24

Faith, Energy and Trust

After becoming interested in spiritual healing one wants to know all the ins and outs of how it works, why it seems to work on some people and not others, why some healers are stronger than others, and a myriad of other doubts and questions. And as we progress further it seems that each answer we get to our questions leads to more questions. Our human nature makes us very inquisitive and we do query how things work, how things happen. But let's be realistic; we cannot possibly understand how many things work and are put together—nobody can. So it really comes back to having a basic faith or belief, doesn't it, and a trust in a good result.

I mean, if you go to the doctor with a flu virus, it is most likely that he will prescribe a course of antibiotics. When this is done you don't sit there and say to him, "Thanks Doc, can you tell me how the anti-biotic knows what to do? How does it work? Do you know?" If you visit the dentist, you don't question how and what he proposes to do to rid you of the bad tooth, do you? No! Of course you don't. We have a faith and a trust in the therapist and believe that he can help us.

When we jump in our car to go to work, we put the key in the ignition and turn it and the car starts. Do we need to know all the ins and outs as to how the engine works, how the car electrics work, etc.? No, of course we don't—it's not necessary to know. We only know the basics—which I believe is all we really need to know. As humans in this physical world, we only need to know the basics of how spiritual healing works. We really are so very lucky, for behind us all the time we have an intelligence far, far greater than our own, to direct and to organise the healing: our helpers in spirit.

I do believe that what we need is 5% knowledge and 95% faith and trust.

Because we are a spirit that takes on human form, and we believe that God, from whom all healing comes is also Spirit, then it stands to reason that the Spirit of God will be able to help the Spirit of man.

Thus put quite simply, all true spiritual healing works in a very simple and basic way.

The healing energy transference can be quite simply said to be:

a) From Spirit   From its divine source—God
b) Through Spirit   Using the healer, who has the gift of healing, and is attuned to Spirit.
c) To Spirit   Received by the spirit of the patient to charge their battery and to send the healing energy to wherever it needs to go.

If someone asks you how it works, use the idea of the power station. For example:

1) The Power Station   Electricity is generated in the power station in its very powerful form, it is then transmitted to—
2) The Transformer   Where the electricity is stepped down in power to a manageable form then passed on to—
3) The Receiver   Which is your house, so that when you switch on the TV, it works OK because the energy is right for the appliance you use.

The spiritual healing energy flows from the spirit of the healer to the spirit of the patient using the chakra or energy centres, which interact between healer and patient. Thus the healing act becomes not only an interaction between two people but also an interaction between two chakra/energy systems.

Please try at all times to keep things in perspective. Spiritual healing is and always has been a very simple act of laying on of hands, and a faith and trust that the act of healing is not being done by us in the physical world but by a far higher intelligence in the spirit world.

For what is faith, unless it is to believe what you cannot see!

I once asked my guides if they could tell me how spiritual healing worked—for I would like to be able to tell people. Their reply was, "Of course we could explain how it works to you. But you wouldn't understand it. For it is beyond human comprehension. You know son, you must all have more trust." How true!

My spirit guides are always emphasising to me that I should trust more. I find it very hard, being a person who wants to be in control and to do things my way, to find this trust. I do believe it takes time and many mistakes until we gradually learn to let go. I don't mean just sitting on our backsides and waiting for it to happen. What I feel is needed is for us to just get on with our lives; try to put action into operation and when we are faced with a situation that we feel we cannot handle, give it our best shot and then simply ask for help. Admit that we don't quite know how to handle the situation and just ask for help. My own experiences have been that things work out the way Spirit want them to and not the way we humans do.

I should like to say in conclusion, don't waste your energy trying to analyse things; trust more and it will happen for you slowly but surely.

Remember, "Only when the pupil is ready, will the teacher arrive."

25

Self Esteem and Self Healing

Aren't we humans funny people, we show a face to the world which puts across to others how very capable and strong we are. But in many cases it's a front, because behind that mask there is often a very insecure and frightened person. The very fact that we are living in the most materialistic society the world has known must add to this situation. It seems that one has to try to impress one's friends and neighbours at all times. This in turn creates stress and unhappiness.

I have seen many people change their lives by becoming interested in spiritual healing and becoming a healer. I do believe it is because they have now found their true vocation, their destiny, and are doing something that they want to do. Now I am not saying that becoming a spiritual healer is the panacea for everyone's ills, but I have seen people change dramatically once they have become involved and started to follow a more spiritual way of life in preference to the material.

I believe I can speak with authority, when I say that nearly everyone who becomes a healer has had much hardship and many problems to overcome during their life. I know I have. It is a question I always ask people who attend my courses, and the answer is always the same. Another question asked of people is, do they feel confident and adequate when dealing with other people. The answer that comes back so many times is that most people lack self-esteem and confidence. The big majority are women, but that's not surprising as the great majority of spiritual healers are women, and it is probably the first time that many of them have really had to be out there meeting people, and once they overcome this minor problem, they progress to become wonderful caring and compassionate healers.

So let us look at 'self esteem'. Self-esteem is the core feeling that you have for yourself as a person; your inner feelings of self-worth, self-love and self-respect.

Self-esteem is the self-affirming consciousness of a mind that trusts itself, and reflects your judgement of your ability to cope with all the challenges and problems of life.

Material possessions, sexual conquests, fine clothes, flashy cars may all make us feel good and satisfy our ego. But this is not self-esteem. These are only very shallow, plastic illusions.

Self-esteem is really not 'what others think of you', for you can be loved by others and not love yourself, or admired by others and yet have a low opinion of yourself. You can project that outer image of self-confidence yet feel lost and unwanted inside.

One can win every accolade yet feel empty inside.

We need to find an inner peace and happiness, for if we do not have this, then it matters not what we have in material wealth or possessions, we shall never be truly happy. Try to take each day at a time; live for the now. Do not worry about the future, in fact do not worry about anything. Let go of the worry and concern, let go of the past; what has gone cannot be changed. Enjoy each day that you have. Try to help others and Spirit will help you. You can be sure of that.

Always remember that your spirit friends are always close to you, to help you, for they love you, more than you can possibly imagine.

26

Symptoms of Disease

Disease or disharmony can occur on different levels, for we are not only a physical body but also mind and spirit. As these three aspects interact with each other, so disharmony can also have this interaction. If a person is under great emotional (mind) stress so the effect may show in the physical (body). For example, an ulcer in the stomach most likely would stem from a person worrying too much about something.

When the unconscious within us is trying to get our attention, it may do so through any of the following symptoms of disease (disharmony).

Disease acts on different levels:

Level	Indication
Physical	Colds, Flu, low energy, increased use of drugs, alcohol, and cigarettes.
Emotional	Depression, edgy, mood fluctuations, crying for no apparent reason, argumentative.
Mental	Being forgetful, making more mistakes, unable to concentrate, lack of self-esteem.
Spiritual	Feeling isolated, cut off from everyone and everything, feeling of no-one cares or understands, feeling very alone.

One needs always to be very careful not to jump to conclusions but to try to cross-reference any symptoms you see, so that you are in a better position to help the person.

27

The Endocrine (Ductless) Gland System

When we look at our human body, we are looking at what we could say was a perfect creation designed by God the creator. A system in which every part works in conjunction with another, so that the body functions perfectly. I don't wish to go into it in any more detail but just ask you to pause for a while to consider the human body and you will marvel at how it all works perfectly—think about it!

One of the processes which serves the body are the endocrine glands, which the ancients in the Hindu and Buddhist religions recognised as primary regulators of both the physical and the spiritual being.

These glands are very important and were seen as the physical equivalent of the main seven chakras or 'energy centres'. Each gland is situated close to one of these energy centres and works in complete harmony with the appropriate centre to which it relates.

The important point to remember is that the energy centres and the glands interact with one another to enable balance to be maintained in the body.

The diagram on page 69 shows the general location of the chakras and the endocrine glands. As you can see, they are located close to each other. Because the chakras and glands are so inter-related, energy passing through the energy centre would have a stimulating affect on the respective endocrine gland.

Some Functions of the Endocrine Glands

This is not meant to be a medical journal and so I don't feel the
necessity to delve too deeply into the subject. Experience tells
me to keep things very basic, so I intend to try and impart a brief
understanding of the contribution that the glands play in everyday
life. The rest we leave to our spirit friends to take care of, whilst
we are in the healing mode.

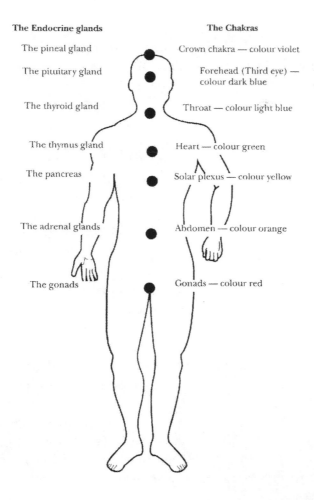

The Endocrine glands

The pineal gland

The pituitary gland

The thyroid gland

The thymus gland

The pancreas

The adrenal glands

The gonads

The Chakras

Crown chakra — colour violet

Forehead (Third eye) — colour dark blue

Throat — colour light blue

Heart — colour green

Solar plexus — colour yellow

Abdomen — colour orange

Gonads — colour red

Picture 4. Location of the endocrine glands and the chakra/energy centre system.

The Pineal Gland	Situated close to the optic nerve area controls and transforms our hormones. Operates in a pacifying role for bodily functions.
The Pituitary Gland	The Pituitary is said to be the master gland, for it has much influence over other glands. Situated at the base of the brain. It could be seen as a sort of receiver channelling all frequencies. It stimulates growth hormones and influences sexual development.
The Thyroid Gland	This Gland sits in the neck area and balances the hormones which affect our growth rate, and keeps a balance in the body. Regulates iodine in the body. Balance of chemicals produced is necessary for the body to perform its functions in harmony.
The Thymus Gland	The Thymus Gland is situated close to the heart, and has an important role in the immune system of the body. The Thymus works in conjunction with the spleen and the lymphatic system. Produces lymph cells used in the blood and lymph system to protect the body.
The Pancreas Glands	The Pancreas Gland near the Solar Plexus controls the digestive system and directs the liver to release sugar into the blood stream. Produces insulin and converts glucose to glycogen to enable the body to store sugar in the system. Deficiencies may cause Diabetes.

The Adrenal Glands	These Glands are located near the kidneys and secrete adrenalins, the fight or flight hormones. Control the heart beat, and any stress conditions that may lead to illness. Responsible for water substance in the body. Converts fats and proteins into carbohydrates.
The Gonads	Situated in the area of our sexual organs, the ovaries and testicles. Hormones here are responsible for our sexual urge and development and the reproductive cycle.

28

The Chakra or 'Energy Centre' System

We understand that the spirit (which is energy) is the life force, which animates the human body. Vitally necessary to this life force energy and its passage in and around the physical body are what in the eastern religions are called chakras, and in the western world are referred to as the 'energy centres'. These centres allow energy to circulate in and out and monitor the flow of energy. So that we can keep to the idea of making it easier for budding healers to work with these centres, without becoming too technical and confused, I intend to look at the basics of what is a very complex subject, and try to condense it into an easily understood approach.

Suffice to say that each book you read will have differing views and information on chakras/energy centres. It is more important for you to have some understanding of where they are situated and the part they play in spiritual healing.

The diagram on page 69 shows the approximate location of each chakra/energy centre, aligned with the spine. Each endocrine gland is situated close to one of these centres. For example the thyroid gland is situated in the threat area, close to the throat chakra centre.

The colours noted are only a reference; for whilst each Chakra is associated with a differing energy, the level of spiritual development is different in each person. It is very interesting to note that the colours associated with the chakra/energy centres are the colours of the rainbow.

Inter-acting with the physical body is the more refined body known as the etheric body which is vibrating at a much higher frequency.

The etheric body contains an energy blueprint upon which the physical body is shaped, and thus they are closely linked. The etheric body is linked directly with our spiritual side of life and contains structures which allow us to absorb the high frequency spiritual energy. Because the etheric permeates the physical body, physical sickness is often picked up in the aura of a person before the physical symptom is evident. The etheric body with its chakra system transforms the healing energy and passes it through to the physical body.

The chakras are joined to an etheric channel aligned with the spine which links the chakras and allows incoming energy to be transformed and passed on to another. As spiritual energy moves through the etheric channels the energies are refined.

We have seven main chakras and a multitude of minor ones, which in Chinese medicine are referred to as acupuncture points. The energies are passed through the chakras and travel throughout the human body by way of 'meridians'.

These meridians, or lines of energy go to all parts of the body, carrying the energies. A study of Shiatsu or reflexology would enhance your knowledge of the energy system of the body. Each of the main chakras is aligned to a major endocrine gland and they work in harmony together.

The power and quality of a healers ability can be directly related to the development and refinement of their chakra System and to their Spiritual development. Our spirit guides will have been working in a very subtle way, all the time leading you to the moment when you begin your healing work. Don't forget! You chose to do the work in this world and your spirit friends also made the agreement to work with you.

They will be responsible for most of your development and refinement on the spiritual level so that you can best serve as a channel for the healing energy to flow through you from Spirit.

As man can direct a physical force so it must be Spirit only that can and does direct the spiritual force (energy). As you develop spiritually your motives and your thoughts will change, bringing a more balanced approach into your life. You will become a clearer channel for Spirit to work with.

The role of the healer during the healing act is to make their conscious mind become essentially passive and to bring the healing energies through by attuning to the higher Spirit Mind, allowing it to become more dominant; to allow the energy to flow through with the minimum of obstruction, using the chakra system, guided to where it is needed by our spirit guides.

Spiritual healing becomes an interaction between two people but mainly an interaction between two chakra/energy systems.

There are now many books you can buy which cover the subject of chakras or energy centres in great detail. Books may vary in their interpretation, so I would advise against trying to become too technical and analytical in your approach to healing.

My own feelings are that the more simple and humble our approach to spiritual healing is, the better channel we will be, and thus the quality of healing will be enhanced. The higher intelligence, which works through us, knows all about such things and is more than capable.

Dear reader: simply have Faith!

29

The Aura

Surrounding the physical body is an energy field, a radiance of varying width, depending on the individual. The aura can only be seen clairvoyantly, it is not visible physically. The aura is composed of varying colours of which the brightness and density or otherwise indicate the condition of the person's bodily, mental and spiritual state.

To give an example: if a person is suffering from a complaint or is physically stressed, depressed etc., and their health is at a low ebb, then the colours shown in the aura would be dull and heavy. On the other hand if the person is quite healthy and well balanced the colours shown in the aura would be bright and sparkling.

The total aura often appears as an oval shape surrounding the body and can extend quite a long way outside the body, and depending on the individual will show a range of colours. It is said that there are seven levels or layers, which inter penetrate each other and vibrate to different frequencies.

In the centre is the physical body, and immediately surrounding this is the etheric body, which is regarded as a blue print of the physical body. Next is the astral or emotional body and outside this are three mental planes bodies, namely instinct, intellectual and spiritual, which contains our thoughts and beliefs. Beyond this is the spiritual body.

Whilst seeing the aura is relatively rare, many people can feel the human energy field. The aura of an average person appears to extend a few inches from the body. Persons who are more spiritually developed, for example healers, tend to have a larger and brighter aura, which projects further from the body, especially around the head. When the early artists placed a halo around the heads of Jesus Christ, the saints and other holy people, I believe they were interpreting the aura.

Because the aura can only be seen clairvoyantly one must be very careful in diagnosing illness by way of the aura; for we must be aware that there are also different qualities and levels of clairvoyant ability. To sum up—the aura is no more than an energy field which gives an image or reflection of a person's spiritual, physical and mental state.

In the past a theory developed that the cause of ill conditions could be taken away by healing the aura, as the healing energy passes through the aura, thus cleansing the aura. It must be acknowledged that the aura is a reflection of the person's state of health, and one cannot heal a reflection.

For those people who wish to do more study on the aura there are books that are solely devoted to this subject. The fact that the aura is only seen clairvoyantly leads to many differences of opinion being given. As with all areas of the psychic or spiritual realm we need to be very perceptive in the way we approach the subject.

30

Preparation and Change

People become involved in spiritual healing for a great variety of reasons and in many different ways. It has been said that our life is planned and that before we are born into this world we choose our parents, our situation and time and place to be born. The lessons we come here to learn and the work we have chosen to do for Spirit are also decided. All these decisions are worked out in conjunction with our management in Spirit.

Once we arrive here in this world, it is as if all is then blocked off from us, and so we proceed to live our life on earth. Because of commitments of marriage, children, careers and other priorities, many don't become interested in spiritual healing until later in life. Once children are off our hands, careers are looked at in a different light, and we have more time on our hands, we start to think about things we want to do for ourselves. Many of you will have had some sort of inner feeling about helping people, some sort of urge to try to change things in the world. This urge, this feeling, doesn't go away. It seems always to be there! I do believe that it is Spirit working on you, working on another level of your conscious. Changes are occurring in you, very slowly and very subtly, over a long period of time. If the job you agreed to do was healing, then from very early on Spirit will be preparing you for the work. They understand all too well your commitments and patiently wait for the right time to come—for it is said, "Only when the pupil is ready, will the teacher arrive." All is known by Spirit and they gently and patiently put the plan into operation and they must prepare you for the work to come.

When one talks to many healers they will tell you they have had many setbacks and many problems to solve in their lives. Most likely you yourselves will also say that your life so far has not been an easy one. Most healers have had many experiences, both good and bad, and I suspect much heartache has occurred. All has been part of a preparation to enable you to do the work with more compassion and empathy. Think about it, had you yourself not suffered much, how could you have empathy and compassion for someone else? You couldn't, could you?

Healers must have an open mind and also have an 'open heart', for it is with love we give healing, and the power of love is so very powerful. Our spirit friends tell us that love is the mightiest force in the universe.

Do not be concerned if you find that changes are occurring with your emotional side, that you feel yourself becoming more emotional at certain times. Maybe you tend to have a few tears where previously you may not have. Changes are being made to you. Maybe you tend now to speak out over such things as the environment, or the injustices in the world, where previously you may have not said anything. That inner urge, call it what you like, just won't go away, will it? Changes are befalling you, things in your life are fluctuating, you are searching for something, you may not be aware yet of what it is you are looking for. You may visit a clairvoyant who tells you about your healing ability, you may go to a spiritualist church and learn more. Maybe it is an advert in the paper which catches your attention, or a friend tells you of books which you should read, or lectures to attend. An advertised course suddenly pops up—all manner of things can happen to direct you to the source.

We don't call these things coincidence, we say rather that Spirit have directed you; it's part of the preparation. I am sure that each of you who are reading this book would have a story to tell as to how you became interested in spiritual healing. So accept changes that manifest in you, know that it is part of the preparation you will undergo. It doesn't stop once you are doing healing work—it keeps on keeping on.

"They who suffer much will know much."

31

Man's Invisible Bodies (Refined Energies)

We have agreed that we human beings are not only a physical body, we are also blessed with a mind and a spirit. Through ancient teachings which have been handed down, and more recent research, we conclude that the human being consists of other refined energies, each of which is vibrating at a different rate and each inter-relates with the other. I do not wish to get too technical on this subject which could lead to confusion. As always I like to put things in a way that is as easy to understand as possible.

Each book you read will no doubt differ in its opinions and details on this complex subject and so I believe it is only necessary to have a basic understanding, because any healing work that needs to be done on other bodies as well as the physical body will be carried out by our healing guides in Spirit and so we should leave all to them.

First is the physical body, which is the manifestation of the life force. The physical body, being solid, vibrates at a lower rate than the other bodies. This body consists of millions of cells, which contain genetic information vital to the workings of the whole body. Subtle changes which may occur even with our other invisible bodies can cause disharmony or disease to occur in the physical body because of the interaction between all levels.

Orthodox medical practice deals with the physical body, whereas spiritual healing, because our spirit doctors control it, may if they feel the necessity be performed on another level. Again it is for them to decide; don't concern yourself with it. It is a matter of technique and is controlled by Spirit.

The second body is called the vital body, the electric field that is an exact subtle blueprint of the physical body. We also call this the 'etheric body' and this is the controller and simulator of energies, which interact with the more dense physical body. All energies are transformed and pass through the chakra/energy centres by which the etheric and physical bodies are linked. It has been said that the etheric body is the archetypal pattern from which the physical body is moulded and that it vitalizes all life forms.

The third body we refer to as the astral body, often referred to as the psychic body or emotional body. Humans are said to be emotional beings and thus it is at this level of our whole self that much healing is done. You will no doubt have heard of astral travel in conjunction with 'out of body experiences', in which it appears that the spirit leaves the physical body for a short period and travels off using the astral body.

The fourth body is said to be tripartite, or three distinct parts, and we say it is the 'mental body'. The three minds, the conscious, the sub-conscious and the super conscious are represented here, as are all activities associated with them. We call each part an aspect in itself—thus the fourth level is three autonomous bodies.

Last but not least we have the soul/spirit body of which we must agree we know very little, for much of the function of the spirit is beyond our comprehension. It is said that the soul or spirit is the seat of our intuition and thoughts connected with knowledge. I think it best if we simply leave this area of our being more in the area of our trusts, our faith and beliefs. Our involvement with these features of the human being is I believe best left to our spirit guides to control, for their knowledge is far higher than our own. It is necessary for us as healers to have an understanding only of the complex structure of us physical beings.

32

Striving for Balance

We have spoken about the need for us humans to have harmony or balance in our lives. In other words we have to nurture and care for ourselves.

There are three kinds of illness which can affect us, we have:

* The Physical
* The Mental
* The Spiritual

Let us look at each one in turn and see how we can understand their implications.

Physical illness is due to infectious diseases, problems of toxicity, and accidents. We must be watchful of the foods that we eat and how much and what we drink. Be aware of not overdoing physical work and avoid smoking, for this can cause much harm to the body. In our everyday life we should try to avoid fatty foods, over indulgence in alcohol and cigarettes, and above all aim for moderation in all things.

Mental illness is caused by fear, anger and worry, all our emotional aspects. It is very true that when a person suffers from any of these emotional problems, the problem will cause a reaction in the physical body. The cause may be on the mental level but the effect will show in the physical, and it is said that 80% of sickness is on this mental or emotional level. Meditation to still the mind, or sitting quietly listening to a favourite piece of music, can have a calming influence on the mind and will help us to attain an inner peace. Being assertive and taking charge of our lives will help us. Try to approach life's problems in a calm, understanding manner. Negative emotions can destroy us and will most definitely create illness within us.

Spiritual sickness is caused by mankind's pursuit of material possessions; his self centredness and greed for money and power. We must not be ignorant of our relationship with God and all that this encompasses. We must be less material and much more spiritual in our outlook on life. By putting self last and serving our fellow man, we shall be helping the coming of harmony into our lives. We must rise above our desires.

We must nurture not only the body but also the Spirit. By maintaining this balance in all aspects of our body-mind-spirit; harmony will be restored ensuring good health for the individual.

Aim for the middle path in all things.

A Simple Example

To illustrate the point, we could use something with which we are all familiar—a flower in your garden

For a flower to grow it needs to have:

A) Sunshine
B) Water
C) Fertiliser or nutrients

It needs each in proportion to the other for the plant to grow.

For if we give the flower lots of sunshine, plenty of fertiliser and no water—it will die. So you can see it needs a balance of all three for the plant to grow properly.

It is surely the same with us humans, wouldn't you agree?

33

Being Aware

When you start to explore some of the many spiritual aspects that confront you in your life you will hear people use the word enlightenment. Some people see this as the pinnacle of spiritual achievement. Other people liken life to a type of spiritual odyssey with enlightenment the final reward. But who really can say what enlightenment is, it is different things to different people. Surely it is the journey which matters the most, and all the experiences and learning that take place on that journey. For I believe that there is no end to that journey, for we are learning all the time. If we are materialistic in our outlook we shall collect possessions along our journey. If we are more spiritual in our outlook we shall collect experiences along the journey. When the time comes when we leave the physical world to go into the Spirit Realm, all material possessions are left behind, and all that can go with us is those experiences we have undergone on our journey.

If we look at Chambers Thesaurus under the word *enlightenment,* we see that it can mean the following: awareness, insight, open-mindedness, understanding, comprehension or learning

When we can see it put in more simple terms it does make it much easier for us to understand. So let us not get too confused trying to analyse what it is; let us find it in our own way, in our own time, by any process that feels comfortable to us.

Every experience is a link in our chain of development.

The more we understand about healing, the more experience we gain in being used as an instrument or channel for that healing energy to flow through us. We learn that the act of Healing (laying on of hands) is and always has been a very simple act. We know that the healing energy comes through the healer and is not of the healer. We know that the healer does not possess more knowledge of how to eradicate disease and sickness than all of our medical scientists and consultants in today's world. And thus when a so called incurable is made well by visiting a healer, we must surely accept that this healing, this change in the patient's condition, can only have been brought about by the intervention of a much higher intelligence than our human one. I call this our spirit guides, God's ministers of healing, who are able to see each healing as a planned act, with intention and direction and, using a healer who has the gift of healing, are able to direct spirit energy, through that healer to help to alleviate suffering in our physical realm. The more we are able to eliminate the human element (our ego, our analysing mind, our doubts etc.) the stronger will the attunement with our spirit friends become, and thus the healing we are doing will also become stronger and we shall be able to help more people to become free of the disease (disharmony) they have in their lives.

34

God and Humankind

As physical man and woman, we humans are a unique species. The bible tells us that God formed us personally by breathing the breath of life into us and created us "in his own image". No other species on earth was given this special gift, which surely would signify that we were to forever enjoy a special relationship with God.

Physically, human life is not very different from that of animals; a bio-chemical existence is common to both. We humans however have a very important extra dimension to our make-up for God, the Creator, bestowed upon human beings a mind, and it is this capacity which makes us unique amongst all God's creatures. The very fact that God (Spirit) gave us this gift which makes the connection with the spirit realm possible does, I feel, reinforce the fact that we do have a spiritual connection with God the Creator.

Human beings are endowed with a spiritual element, which gives them a unique mental dimension: to know and to comprehend human things, and to be able to think, to reason, to determine and to create.

The spirit in man enables us to comprehend the world around us; this is the real you! All our thoughts, our consciousness, our feelings, our hopes and dreams are contained in this spirit mind. It would appear then that the mind is independent and superior to the brain and must be non-physical and non-material in its aspect. All has been formed by God and is of the Spirit. The Spirit is the life force which motivates the human form.

I use the word God in regard to healing for it is what I have been brought up with. Nobody can explain God, or what God is. It is beyond our comprehension. Some of you may wish to use cosmic energy, universal energy, an all knowing entity or whatever words you may feel comfortable with. Please know that this is all right; I'm sure the power that is will be more concerned with your motives than the name you give to it.

35

Balance in our Lives

It is most important that we endeavour to keep a balance in our lives, the way we look at life and the way we react to everyday happenings, for if we do not then sickness will occur. We say that we are not just a physical body, but also possess a mind and a spirit, and we should always try to ensure that each of these is also in harmony.

Let us look at our physical body and know that we must look after it and not abuse it. The physical body enables us to walk, run, swim, lift weights and play all manner of games and a host of other activities. Bear in mind that we must always apply common sense and restraint in regard to the use of our bodies. Never over extend the body. All sports people have a warming up period prior to any activity, which allows the body to prepare itself for future stress. As we get older we must realise that we cannot do with our bodies the things we used to do when younger. Performance enhancing drugs will not do our bodies any good whatsoever, so don't use them. Remember to keep that balance when dealing with the physical body. Looking after it will be of great benefit in your later life.

Let us look now at the mind, and we have to say that this is an area about which little is known or understood. We could say that the mind is responsible for all our thoughts, either negative or positive. So we must keep a perspective here, we must try to think more positively in our lives and not let negative thoughts take over. If we become very negative we become depressed and make ourselves ill. If we allow too much stress and worry into our minds this in turn will make us ill. Worry over something can make a person either overeat or not eat enough. This also will lead to ill health. If we can keep a sense of balance in our lives, and in our minds, then we can to a great extent alleviate the sickness and disharmony in our lives.

If we do not allow the spiritual side of us to develop, if we ignore it, and we close it down and we become too materialistic in our outlook, we shall suffer stress, which will make us ill. The spiritual aspect of each of us needs to be nurtured; it is there, it is part of us, it is our destiny and as such needs to be developed. Remember to keep a balance: do not forsake your normal everyday life, your commitments to family, work etc. and blindly pursue the spiritual search. Have a bright outlook in all that you do. I do believe this is what God intended us to do.

If we look at nature, we see balance in all things. Every plant, every insect, fish or animal, plays its part. The seasons, the tides, the rising and setting of the sun, all play their part in God's handiwork.

A perfect plan which we humans fit into; unfortunately, as with many things that mankind touches, we tend to create havoc. God's plan is perfect; there is a reason for everything. If we were to take out of the system the bees and butterflies, no plants or flowers would be pollinated—thus no fruit and no plants—so no food for our animals and birds, which rely on those plants, and so we humans would also suffer—again chaos.

So remember to live a balanced life!

* If we work too many hours and don't sleep enough, we make ourselves ill.
* If we worry too much and don't use our common sense, we shall make ourselves ill.

*   If we don't take charge of our own lives but let others control us, or if we pursue material possessions and forget our Spiritual side, we shall make ourselves ill.

Realise that it is you and only you that controls your life and what you do with it. Once you take charge and put things into their right perspective, changes for the better will occur.

36

Principles of Coordination

Our physical body is a wonderful, well planned, perfect vehicle for our spirit to use during its sojourn on the earthly plane. Every part of our physical body has its place and its function, and all work together in harmony and perfect balance. That is, of course, unless we humans abuse or mistreat our bodies. If we have moderation and balance in all we do, we would see that our physical body would perform as was intended, and so we should look after it.

For it has been said: *The body is the temple of the Spirit.*

Let us look at the systems that work within this temple, and what function they perform, and how we can best help matters.

Digestive system. We should try to eat the right foods; lots of fruit and vegetables, nutritional foods, and not too much fat. Try to drink less alcohol or soft drinks, and drink more water, as this does help to clean out the system. Aim for a balanced diet.

Circulatory system. Try to get lots of exercise; walking and swimming are good for you as they help to get the blood flowing throughout the body. Have a massage regularly. Be careful not to over exert the body.

Respiratory system. Breathe in fresh air deeply when exercising, for the oxygen we breathe invigorates the blood in our bodies. Get plenty of sunshine, maybe a walk in the fresh country air away from the traffic fumes of the cities. Stop smoking, for as you know this does endanger your health.

Immune system. The body's immune system controls our health, and acts as a guardian to keep out the nasties, providing protection for the body. Try to keep a positive outlook on life, relax more, laugh more, and look to the future with confidence. Do not worry and do not allow yourself to get run down or stressed out.

Endocrine glands system. Our glands are very important to our health, for they act as a sort of regulator to keep a balance in the physical body. The less stress we put ourselves under, the better our glands will function. The endocrine glands work in close conjunction with our chakras or energy centres. Try to aim for a more stress free life.

The nervous system. The nervous system supplies life energy to the brain, heart and all other major organs, and to all parts of the body. It distributes energy to the five senses of smell, touch, taste, sight, and feeling, and is our channel for contact with the world through our sensory reactions.

All these systems work in conjunction, to create a balance in the body, and so good health will follow. The main principle of good health is to try for moderation in all things. We know that we will have our ups and downs, the negatives and positives in life, but always remember: if we did not experience the depressions (lows), we would not be able to appreciate the serenity and contentments (highs).

37

Code of Conduct

When I have discussed spiritual healing with doctors and others in positions of authority they have all been impressed by the extent and details of my training and experience, and the fact that healers do work with a code of conduct. The latter shows that we are a credible, genuine group of people who are proud of our gift and working towards having spiritual healing recognised as a genuine healing therapy. I am going to refer again to the National Federation of Spiritual Healers (UK) who, in their wisdom, and showing great foresight, asked the British Medical Association to help them to draw up a Code of Conduct that spiritual healers could work by. This was refined and put into operation and is now the guideline which many spiritual healing groups use to direct and assist their members.

Whilst I don't intend to set out the whole document, I shall explain that it is for the most part a matter of commonsense and, as such, acts as a protection for those who abide by the instructions set out in the article.

I should like to briefly give some examples to show you the general emphasis behind the Code.

1. All N.F.S.H. Healer Members must agree to abide by the Code of Conduct and this demonstrates to the medical profession and the patient the healer's integrity, sincerity and ability.
2. Healers must strive to maintain a good relationship with doctors; we must recommend new patients to a doctor,

and we must not countermand a doctor's instructions. We healers do not diagnose; we must seek to be a complement, and not an alternative, to medical treatment.

3. When visiting hospitals we must at all times act with discretion, seeking permission from the Ward Sister and not undermining the hospital in any way, for they are responsible for the patients' welfare.

4. Healers are responsible for their actions and should behave with courtesy, dignity and tact at all times.

5. Healers must not give guarantees of a cure.

6. Healers must not give clairvoyant readings during healing.

7. Be very aware when giving healing to a member of the opposite sex privately, of where you place your hands. It is very advisable to have a third party present as a safeguard.

8. Healers must not use manipulation or vigorous actions when healing.

9. Under no circumstances should a healer give a medical diagnosis. Diagnosis is the sole responsibility of a doctor.

10. Healers must treat as confidential all information of a personal nature, which has been confided by the patient.

11. Healers must keep adequate confidential records for all patients.

This is just a very brief summary of the N.F.S.H. Code of Conduct, but it serves to give you an idea as to what is required.

A code of conduct is very important for all healers to abide by. Make sure that any person or group that you consider joining does aim for high moral values.

So in summarising, let me say this:

1. Read books on spiritual healing with your mind open, and accept what you are comfortable with.

2. Seek out any groups in your area, check them out to see if you feel comfortable with them. Ask questions and follow your intuition.

3. Once you have found a group, then look at the idea of doing a course on spiritual healing.

4. Practice your healing. I suggest that you could start with your family, friends, etc. Be patient; the group you join can help here.

5. You will meet other people of like mind and form friendships. This in turn will open other doors for you. Remember:

Only when the Pupil is ready can the Teacher arrive.

38

Body, Mind and Soul

Much has been said of the fact that we are a spirit with a human physical body and not a body with a spirit. It is the spirit which is the 'life force' for our physical body, and the spirit which animates the physical body. Once the spirit leaves the body, never to return, death occurs, because the life-force energy has gone. To give an analogy, when a car runs out of petrol it stops. The petrol provides the energy that keeps the car going. When the tank is empty it will not go.

Linking the spirit and the physical is the mind. The mind acts as the bridge between Spirit and physical.

Physical body — — — — — — — — — — — — — — **Spirit body**
— **Mind** —

As human beings we possess a physical or conscious mind which is concerned with the material things we do in our daily life. This mind sorts out information and is responsible for the—shall we call them mundane—actions and thoughts: "The sun is hot today, what movie am I going to see tonight? What's for tea tonight? What shall I cook?" The conscious mind passes all to the brain, our human computer, which then acts on the information supplied.

Our spirit mind is also an analytical mind, concerned with the spiritual side of life; our feelings and emotions, our conscience and our spiritual development, because it is in harmony with the spirit realm. When we wish to link with Spirit for spiritual healing to begin, we need to relax and seek that inner peace and tranquillity. Our spirit mind then needs to gain ascendancy as we concentrate on spiritual thoughts. We then seek for the physical mind to become less and less in control so that the spirit mind may take over.

The two minds work together during healing. Information on the patient: physical conditions, mental stress or emotional stress are assessed through the physical (conscious) mind, and then conveyed to the spirit mind which is attuned to the spirit realm. The healing guides in the spirit realm can then act on this information and provide whatever action is necessary.

Every act of healing is a planned act and all results, changes, cures etc., are the result of law governed forces; nothing is by chance.

The energy that is used is a spiritual energy which comes from its divine source, God. It cannot be directed or manipulated by physical beings; it can only be directed by a superior intelligence in the spirit realm, one much wiser than we in the physical world. An intelligence that has acquired the wisdom and knowledge to use this spiritual energy to help heal the sick here on earth, and to create greater harmony and balance in our lives, in all aspects of 'body—mind—spirit'.

39

The Mind Affects the Body just as the Body Affects the Mind

Each time we commence our healing session we need to change from being motivated by the physical mind, as in diagram A, to being motivated by our spiritual mind, as in diagram B.

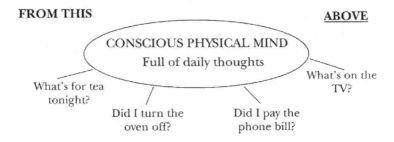

FROM THIS   **ABOVE**

CONSCIOUS PHYSICAL MIND
Full of daily thoughts

What's for tea
tonight?

Did I turn the
oven off?

Did I pay the
phone bill?

What's on the
TV?

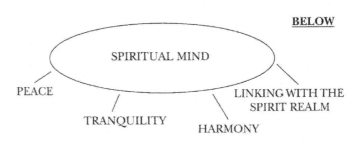

BELOW

SPIRITUAL MIND

PEACE

TRANQUILITY

HARMONY

LINKING WITH THE
SPIRIT REALM

Diagram A

Diagram A

TO THIS

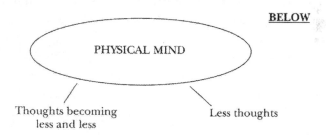

Diagram B

Diagram B

The spirit mind has to become ascendant when we meditate, as this brings the peace and harmony we need to allow our spirit friends to communicate. They cannot communicate through the physical mind, which is full of everyday thoughts, because the channels are not clear. Think of it in this way: if your son or daughter sits with their walkman radio on they cannot hear you and you cannot communicate with them. Our mind should be as clear and free from interference as we can make it.

40

Spirit Guides

The subject of spirit guides, spirit guardian angels, spirit friends, call them what you will, often comes up when I am talking to people who are becoming involved in spiritual healing. With many people it can become a source of ammunition to boost their ego. To show you what can happen, I was listening to a group of people quite new to healing, and one said quite proudly that she had five Spirit Guides working with her; another lady in the group said that she herself had seven. These comments were made solely to impress other people in the group and to boost the speaker's ego. I have met other people who state that they won't make a decision, join a group, buy anything, etc., unless they have checked with their guide first.

I shall never forget a young couple who were in one of my healing courses who told me quite confidently and sincerely that their guide had told them that they were flying back to England, they quoted the date they were leaving the day and even the flight number. They were very sure of these facts and I must admit I thought to myself, "Heck, if they have communication and guidance that good, I am very envious."

The day came and went and I didn't think much about it but waited for a postcard. Three days later they both turned up at the course, looking quite subdued. I didn't rub it in, but spoke openly, and I know they learnt a valuable lesson through it all. They have since gone on to become wonderful healers and are doing great work together.

So let us look at this subject of 'spirit guides'. I should like to impress upon you that the opinions I shall put forward are mine and as such I believe them to be right—but it is for you to accept or reject.

41

Management

I call my spirit friends, my guides, and the healing guides who work with me my 'Management.' I use this word because it is not I that am responsible for the healing. I am but a channel through which the healing energy sent from God, the Divine Source, flows. I want to now break this up into a couple of scenarios, so that we can look in more depth at the question.

Firstly, I would say: if you have incarnated into this life to simply experience various incidents, emotions etc., that will enhance your spiritual growth, then I believe that you will have what I shall call a 'Guardian'.

Some people refer to them as 'guardian angels' and this spirit being will be with you throughout your earthly life. They will walk with you every step of the journey, to assist you and to help you and to try to guide you. But let me emphasise most strongly:

They cannot and will not do it for you.

Many people get this wrong, they think that Spirit will make their decisions and do things for them. Believe me now!

Read my lips—they will not.

God gave us free will and we only learn from trying. We shall make mistakes—but we are always learning. Naturally there are many, many people who are in this situation. I'm sure that you all know plenty. Some will undoubtedly carry on living for the material affluence they covet and may never look at any other way of life. Others, through experiences or happenings in their lives, may turn to people like ourselves as healers for some sort of guidance, and we may be able to sow some seeds with them. It is nevertheless a fact that these people will also have a spirit guardian.

I should now like to turn your attention towards those people like yourselves who are becoming more interested in spiritual healing. All of you no doubt will experience an inner feeling as regards healing, and will be drawn towards the more spiritual aspects of life. This inner urge may take different forms: only you yourself will understand it. I liken it to being on a drug, you just cannot seem to stop it, and it always seems to be there and won't go away. The reason why this inner feeling is so strong, I believe, is because it has come through with you from your previous lifetimes in spirit. Before you incarnated into this life here on earth, it is my belief that you contracted with your spirit colleagues that you would walk the path of a spiritual healer whilst you were here on earth. The 'gift of healing' was given to you; a healing guide was also brought in to work with you. It is most likely that you would have been together in many previous lifetimes and so would be very compatible with each other. Your guide will be well versed in the healing arts.

I am also of the opinion that your life will have a plan to it, a structure of what you will do, and of the people you will meet on your journey. I don't believe that there are 'coincidences', that things happen by chance. I am sure that there is a big plan for us on earth, and it is working slowly and surely in the background. Along with the gift of healing, God also gave us free will (more on this later).

To help you to understand the situation more and to assist you if anyone may ask you about your healing guides, and how it works, I should like to draw your attention to the following simple example.

I would like you to think about this idea the next time you go to see a play at the theatre. On the stage there may be, shall we say, between 3 and 6 people performing their roles. What you don't see are the scores of other people behind the scenes who really worked to make the play possible.

Watch a video, and again you actually see only a few of the people who play a part in the show. When the film ends make sure that you take a look at the credits, and you will see the names and functions of scores more people who made it all possible. All manner of jobs had to be done by hundreds of people to enable a chosen few to perform in front of the camera.

I have tried to draw to your attention these everyday analogies so that you can be clearer on how your spirit management works. This diagram will help you to understand.

When we look at an iceberg floating in the Antarctic Ocean, what do we see?

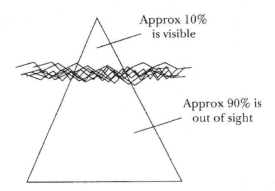

We see only about 10% of its volume. The remaining 90% is hidden below the surface. There is a similar relationship between us and our 'healing management'.

From the point of view of Spirit, the iceberg analogy needs to be turned upside down.

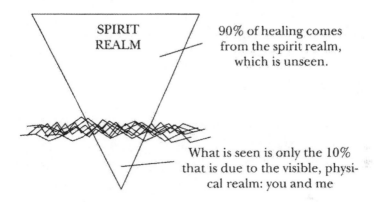

SPIRIT REALM

90% of healing comes from the spirit realm, which is unseen.

What is seen is only the 10% that is due to the visible, physical realm: you and me

We as healers play only a small part in the healing operation, though a vitally important part. All true spiritual healing is controlled by our friends in spirit; they are responsible for all aspects of healing. Any diagnosis needed for directing the spirit energy to enable the healing to take place, and the technique which they wish to be used to effect this healing, is organised by the management.

42

When we commence our healing work

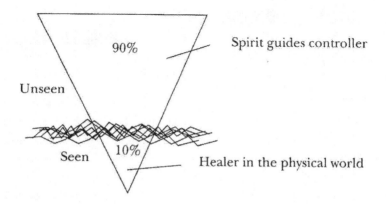

When we commence healing work we will have our healing guide with us and this guide will be in control of all aspects of the work in the spirit realm. Remember we are just starting our healing work and need to work together (spirit guides and healer) so that with practice and much patience we can strengthen and develop our healing gift, to the best of our abilities.

As we develop as a healer, we will attract other healing spirits to us. Our healing guide remains in charge, but can bring in other spirit doctors to work with us. If your healing guide decides that some extra knowledge of a particular illness is required then a more specialised spirit healer will be asked to work through you.

Think of it like your own doctor. What would he do, if he wasn't sure about something? He would refer you to a specialist, one who is an expert in that particular branch of medicine.

This is exactly what happens in the spirit world. If your guide needs a specialist opinion, then that will be organised. So the management looks a bit more like the diagram on the next page. The healers in spirit work well together; there is no ego to please and they work in harmony with each other. Sadly, the same cannot be said for many in this world.

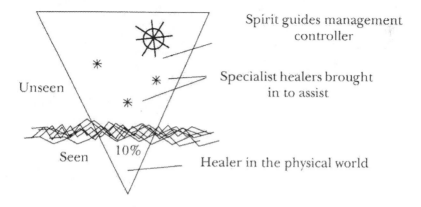

Spirit guides management controller

Specialist healers brought in to assist

Unseen

Seen

10%

Healer in the physical world

All spiritual healing comes from God/Spirit, and we as healers in the physical world play our part in conjunction with God's spirit healers to use this spiritual energy. As we go further into healing and become more experienced we build on the vital attunement between the transmitter of the healing energy—our guides—and the transformer of the Healing Energy—we the healers.

As man can direct a physical force, so it requires a spirit to direct a spirit force/energy. We must therefore conclude that the operating mind behind this act must be a non physical mind. A mind that has acquired a far greater wisdom than us mere mortals, a mind that understands and can control and direct this life force of spiritual energy to help mankind.

As you can see we as the healer play a small part in the healing operation. It is none the less a very important part. Once we lay our hands on to the patient we have a great wealth of knowledge, energy and love behind us all the time, whose one desire is to help us with our healing. Your management is always with you to help and assist. They will never fail you.

For we humans one of the hardest things to do is to 'let go', to let your spirit management do what they do best, and that is to manage. Please allow them to organise the conditions so that the best results can be achieved for the patient.

Have faith, and believe in your management.

43

The Human Element

When we first start to become involved in spiritual healing, with our first laying on of hands on to a patient seated in the chair in front of us, we know, from all that has been instilled in us, that the healing comes from God, from its divine source in the spirit realm. We hope our belief is true, because at this moment of contact with the patient we feel very unsure of ourselves.

Here we are, with our hands on the patient's shoulders, wondering what is to happen next. Our apprehensions, our doubts and fears come flooding in. Gone is the confidence we thought we had. I believe that whilst this can be a fearful situation, it is a very good lesson for us. Something to learn by. I call this the *human element,* and it is quite normal for us to have doubts and uncertainties.

I believe I would be right in saying that all healers have at some time experienced it. If there is one thing I try to do, it is to instil in new healers that they keep out the human element.

Let us take a closer look at this, because I know it will be of a great help to you in your healing future. We understand that we are a mind, physical body and spirit body. We possess a physical mind, which is concerned with the everyday things in life. The spirit mind is concerned with the spiritual, emotional and intuitive things. With spiritual healing it is our spirit mind which has to become superior and override the physical mind.

Let us try to visualise the healer with hands on the patient for that first time. They start to think:

* Is it going to work?
* Does Spirit know I'm here to heal?
* I cannot feel anything happening.
* I wonder if it will work this time?
* How does it work?
* What's going to happen?
* And, I am sure, many other thoughts will pop into your head and you will start to feel very uncertain and fearful.

This is the human element—our conscious mind, our ego, wanting to be in control and not wanting to 'let go'. It is we in the physical world thinking that we know more than our guides in the spirit world.

Keep the human element out of the situation. You have done your preparation to attune with Spirit; start quietly and calmly now. Just place your hands on to the patient and simply ask for help. Believe your spirit doctors are there, always have been and always will be when you do the healing. Have faith in them.

I can honestly say to you that they know more about you than you do yourselves. They know what is wrong and what has to be done to help the patient, as soon as the patient sits in the chair, and as soon as you lay hands on to the patient. So forget your thoughts, put them out of your mind.

Another mistake we make when we start on our journey is like this: We are in a group doing healing. We hear another healer say, "Gee, when I was doing the healing, I felt such and such," or "I saw colours when I was Healing," or "I'm sure I was getting a message through".

Please, please do not worry about this for some people delude themselves. Some get carried away and some do genuinely see or hear. It does not matter for, remember, we are all of us on our own individual journey and we are all exactly where we should be for our development.

Trust your spirit friends. They have everything under control. They are guiding you in the right direction at the right speed.

Another trap we can fall into as beginners is that we watch other healers and see that they may be doing something different to us, and so we think, "Hey! I must be doing it wrong. I'd better do the same as they are doing".

Wrong; do what your teacher has shown you. Beware of those healers who are more for show and effect. Those who flick their hands after passing over the body. Those who draw crosses in the air or the ones who look as though they are plucking things out of the air from around the patient.

All true spiritual healing is, and always has been, a very simple, basic laying on of the hands. Nothing more is needed for successful healings to take place. Certainly not the odd theatrics of some people. Can you imagine the reaction such a person would get were they to go into a hospital ward to do healing in this manner; the ward Sister would give them short shrift.

I must make mention that some healers work by placing the hands close to the patient's body and use this technique in their healing. This is perfectly all right. It is an individual's choice to decide which feels most comfortable to them. But please, no theatrics.

The main point we must remember at all times is that the healing act is controlled by Spirit. We, of course, as Healers, play our part; we in the physical are providing the link between our spirit guides and the patient. Most patients come to us in a stressed condition, suffering physical or emotional pain, and the very fact that we have taken time to listen to their problems and have been able to calm their fears so that they can feel more relaxed and calmer in the mind will help them to be more receptive to the healing energies which will flow through us to them.

As soon as you lay hands on to the patient you have made the link for spirit. You must then hand over to spirit, let them take control, for whatever is going to happen, is in their capable hands. It is at this point that we must keep the negative side of our human element totally out of things. All the preparation has been done and we now say "Thy will be done," and concentrate our conscious mind in sending love, and visualise healing helping to make the person healthy. We should not concern ourselves with diagnosing or any other concerns we may have which will not help the healing in any way.

Remove the human element, the ego, and give over to the spirit intelligences that work through you. Once you can learn to leave the healing techniques and methods of healing to your spirit guides, and understand that it is not you who is doing the healing, then your healing will get stronger, for the attunement between you and Spirit will become better and you will be a much clearer channel for Spirit to work with.

For what is Faith, unless it is to believe what you do not see?

44

Attunement/Harmonising

As healers we are seeking the development of whatever healing gift we have to its highest potential. This can only be obtained by we healers being open to Spirit and really wanting to work for Spirit. We all have healing ability; it is part of our spiritual development. We may have been involved in healing in past lives. It is most likely that the guides we have working with us now have been with us before also. So we have this affinity with our spirit friends. And so as we sit quietly seeking attunement we are building a state of compatibility with our spirit guides. Nothing is by chance; all is ordered, all is known by spirit. The very fact that you are interested in healing is all part of a big plan—known only to Spirit.

All true healing has its basis in Love.

The love that comes to us from spirit can be overwhelming, it is a wonderful feeling which I sincerely hope you will experience.

Love in its highest form, which I call 'spiritual Love', is so far above what we experience as physical love. Unfortunately most people associate love with sex. Love (spiritual Love) is divine.

When we can truly open our heart and let that love from Spirit flow through us, only then will we be true spiritual healers, and only then will we fulfil our destiny and develop that wonderful gift of healing which God gave to us.

The pure heart becomes inspired, uplifted—for it sees beyond intellect and reason.

True attunement with Spirit is as simple as sitting quietly, opening your heart to Spirit and truly meaning it, when you ask to be used as a channel for the healing energy to flow through you to help mankind.

It really is as simple as that, just to ask with your 'heart' for Spirit to use you in whatever way they deem fit, for you are truly ready, willing and able to work for Spirit. To humbly pray for your healing guides to work with you in love. When you can do this you will have attunement/ harmony with your spirit helpers. As you journey along your spiritual path you will have by your side your spirit helpers who are so close to you, even though you may not see them; they will walk every step with you and they will never let you down, for they truly love you.

Hands that help are more blessed—than lips that pray.

I speak from experience in all this, for during my time in healing I have, as they say, 'lost the plot' several times. Each time my guides have been patient with me and shown me love and compassion.

I have been humbled, and have apologised to them for the error of my ways. I have even tried to blackmail Spirit into doing things for me. I have been egotistical and too clever for my own good.

When the crunch finally came I was told by them that they shed tears, for I had a wonderful gift which I was not using to its full potential. They said that they couldn't interfere for it was my choice, my free will. They showed me so much love and understanding—it was an incredible feeling.

Please believe me, fellow healers, that Spirit understand our human frailties; they know what our world is like, and they love you. If you slip off the path they will gently help you back on to the right way. If you truly want to work for Spirit they will work with you, with love.

They know what is in your heart.

For when we love it is the heart that judges and not the head.

45

The Kiss Principle

As I have progressed further into spiritual healing, and have received more guidance from Spirit, it is now becoming so much more defined that the 'Golden Rule' is that it is Spirit who controls every facet of the healing act. Every healing is a planned act, organised, controlled and carried out by Spirit, using us healers in the physical realm as a channel. Spirit tell us time and time again to lose the ego, the human element as I call it. They tell us that healing is a simple act of laying on of our hands on to a patient, asking to be used, and then standing back, so to speak, and allowing the superior knowledge and understanding of those in the spirit realm to commence their work.

Spirit has organised the healing doctors in spirit who will work with you, to be ready to use spirit energy to flow through to the patient. They have attuned their instrument (which is you the healer) to the level that is needed to ensure that the energy force from the Spirit realm (God) will flow smoothly through to the patient. As soon as the patient sits with you whilst you are in counselling mode, and listening to what they are telling you, Spirit will have it all ready, knowing exactly what is needed and, having diagnosed the situation, will be organised ready to begin. All that is needed is for us to lay hands on to the patient, thus making the connection. We ask to be used as a healing instrument and say "Thy will be done," and then leave all to our spirit helpers, who, with their knowledge of energy transfer, know exactly what to do!

Great thoughts come from the heart.

I have visited many places where healing takes place, I have watched many people as they go through the healing act. I have to say that I am amazed at some of the antics I have observed. There are some very good examples of 'showmanship' that should be on the stage. I have seen people standing behind the patient and using their hands in a clawing movement as if they were digging something away from that person. I have witnessed others using their hands in a scooping motion around the patient; I have seen others doing a sort of flicking movement away from the patient.

When I asked innocently what they were doing I was told that they were removing negative energy from the patient. I have observed healers making crosses in the air around the patient. I have seen healers holding their hands about 30 centimetres from the body and using their hands in a stroking motion all around the patient. I was told that they were working in the etheric and healing the aura. I could tell you more but I won't, because I am holding my head in my hands and asking, "What next?".

What would a medical doctor think of healing if he saw these sorts of antics going on. What would a ward sister think of healing if she saw this. Think about it! They would rightly think we were a bunch of crackpots performing, and who could blame them. Any new patient not knowing anything about spiritual healing must also get the wrong idea about what spiritual healing really is. We are trying so hard to get recognition from the medical profession; let's not spoil our chances by showmanship.

I have given this subject a great deal of thought because it is very important for all probationary healers to bear in mind, and in fact it won't hurt for all of us to be aware. If we want to progress in our healing work, to do the best we can, we must lose the ego: forget the showmanship, and get back to what spiritual healing really is: "A basic act of laying on of hands".

To enable us to 'Get back to the basics' I have worked out a basic formula for you to use. We all know what a 'Kiss' is don't we, can you remember, your first kiss! Think how nice a kiss can be. Everyone kisses; its something we don't ever forget how to do.

I call the basic formula the '**KISS** principle'.

Keep!

It!

Simple!

Sincere!

Keep It simple and sincere

You cannot forget that, can you? Of course not.

Let us not insult our spirit friends by kidding ourselves, and any that watch us in the healing act, that we know more than our spirit helpers do. Please don't be so egotistical as to think that you know how best to carry out the healing act. Spirit doesn't tell you to do the theatricals, they don't tell you about the techniques being used because you wouldn't understand what it means. So don't kid yourself you are working in the etheric level, or that you as a human being are able to scoop up spiritual energy. Please put aside the human element, the ego: work with Spirit, doing your part as God intended. Once you can do this, your reward will be that the power and quality of the healing will magnify, for you will be truly a spiritual healer, and don't forget KISS!

Keep it simple and sincere.

The distinguishing qualifications of a master are not physical but spiritual.

46

The Healer's Attitude to the Patient

As you will know, first impressions are usually lasting impressions, and so it is very important that the patient is made to feel welcome, put at ease and made comfortable when they first meet the healer. We should always be aware that the patient is most probably under stress, undergoing emotional problems and maybe even in a depression. They may have been to other places for help and only received drugs, when in actual fact they really needed to talk to someone about their personal problems. It is said that, "A problem shared is a problem halved," and this is very true.

By allowing the patient to talk about their problem, the healer is showing that there is somebody who is prepared to listen. The important point to note here is that you are building a rapport with the patient, which is very necessary for healing to take place. There needs to be an interaction between patient and healer to develop mutual trust, understanding and confidence that all is well and that something good will come out of this session.

A) Meet the patient and greet them with a smile, introduce yourself, make them feel welcome and sit them down in a comfortable chair.

B) Ask how you can be of help, and discuss their problem with them. We need at this stage to take down some details, and so we would fill out their details on a reference card as shown below.

<u>Patients Name:</u> Marilyn Trembath

| Address | City | Postcode | Phone No |
| 6 Sandhurst Rd | Perth | 6059 | 9275 1842 |

| Healer's name | Patient's problem |
| David Clements | Severe migraine & emotional upset |

Date of Healing	Healer	Remarks and Progress
10/10/97	David	Patient felt very relaxed some tears during healing session.
17/10/97	David	Patient says she felt more relaxed when sleeping and more happy
24/10/97	David	Migraine much less severe, patient feeling happier about life, and a more relaxed attitude.

Suitable cards can be obtained from newsagents. It is important that a card is kept for each patient, for your reference and also should another healer have to fill in for you at any time. The card enables them to quickly assess the patient's progress and so they can follow up on what healing has been received with a minimum of fuss.

C) Both the healer and patient need to be seated comfortably in a quiet place, preferably away from other people. Ask them in their own time to tell you what has been happening. Just let them talk while you listen attentively, taking notes if you wish.

D) As a healer, you will hear some very disturbing stories about what some people have suffered. You must not let this affect you. Don't take their problems on board and be conscious of the need to—firstly, avoid passing judgement, and secondly, refrain from giving advice!

E) People may ask you what they should do! Be aware that it is their problem and only they can solve it. You can offer support but do not offer your opinions. If for example they say, "What should I do?" You could then say to them, "What do you feel you want to do?" In other words throw it back to them to make a decision.

F) Sometimes you may have a person come to you who is not very talkative and cannot communicate very well. It may be through nerves or they may not be very good at communicating with others. This often leads to what I call a 'yes-no' conversation and you cannot find out much. If this happens to you, try prefacing your question with one of the following words:

WHEN?

WHERE?

HOW?

WHY?

WHAT?

WHO?

A simple example: "Are you in pain now?"

The patient answers—"Yes!"

Try using: When does the pain feel worse?

How does the pain affect your work?

Where does the pain start in your arm?

By using these words it will help you to get a conversation going.

Be aware that if the patient does not want to talk, that is OK also.

G) Another very important reason for spending some time in communication with a patient is because it will make you aware if that person needs special treatment. I have been to some places of healing where people are told "If you want to have some healing, then go into the other room and be seated and a healer will attend to you!" To my way of thinking this is not a good way of giving healing and totally lacks any feeling of caring or compassion.

A simple example will show how this is.

A woman comes to this place for healing; she is very emotional and nervous. She may have been physically or emotionally abused by her husband. She is told to sit in a room on a chair and wait. Along comes a man, who asks if she would like some healing. No way is this woman going to want any man to lay hands on her, it would be too traumatic. The healing will not take place!

Similarly, there are men who do not feel comfortable with a woman healer, or the patient may prefer someone to heal them from their own ethnic background. You can see how situations like this can occur.

Isn't it much more convenient, as well as showing caring and empathy, to take a little time to communicate with the patient so that all these problems can be sorted out in the beginning. The patient will feel better and go away happier and contented and will definitely return for more healing.

H) Should the healer feel that for whatever reasons the rapport with the patient is not happening, it is advisable to call in the services of another healer in the centre. This should be done without the patient being aware of the situation so as not to cause concern.

For example: The patient may be a woman and the healer a man, so the patient may feel more comfortable explaining her problem to another woman. The male healer, using his intuition, would pick this up and excuse himself by saying something like, "I would like to introduce you to Mary Smith, because I feel she would be able to help you more." He would then explain the situation to Mary and then withdraw discreetly. In closing, I would like to say this to you, that this situation rarely occurs in healing, thank goodness, but one should be aware of it.

As I have explained earlier, the main functions of counselling/communicating with the patient is for the healer to establish a good rapport with the patient, and whilst this is happening, our friends in spirit are preparing the spirit healers for their major part in the healing act, and so when that rapport has been established and the healer lays hands on the patient, it is then 'all systems go'. Spirit then take control and energy flows through from Spirit.

47

Aide-Memoire for Healers

Let us now look at how we can help those healers who are perhaps just commencing their healing career. I call it 'setting the scene', a sort of 'check list' for them to follow to ensure that all will run smoothly.

Firstly many enquiries come by way of the telephone and when that call is received we must be aware that first impressions really do matter greatly. Always be pleasant, and a friendly and warm tone of voice is required. For remember that the person making the inquiry will most likely feel upset and emotional and looking for help. Introduce yourself and ask how you may be of help to them. You will know the times you have available for healing and when you can fit them in and so are well prepared to assist. An enquiry would probably go something like this:

The phone rings; you answer, "Hello, Sunshine Healing Centre, David speaking—how can I help you?"

Caller: "My name is Jean Jackson and I would like to come to see you regarding my depression."

Healer: "OK, that sounds like a good idea. When would best suit you to make an appointment, when are you available?"

Caller: "As I am not working, I could come any time during the day."

Healer: "Just bear with me a moment, I am just checking my diary—how does 10.00 o'clock, this Thursday morning suit you?"

Caller: "Yes! Thank you, that sounds very good. Is it all right if I bring my friend with me?"

Healer: "By all means, bring your friend with you. Do you know our address and how to get here?"

Caller: "Yes I do, thank you."

Healer: "That's good, I look forward to meeting you on Thursday at 10 o'clock. Take care."

Try to keep things fairly brief on the phone. If the patient wants to ask question, etc., I believe it is easier to discuss things when they are with you, on a one to one basis. Any questions of fees or donations can be explained if they are raised by the patient. If you were working from a healing centre then certain specific times would be arranged for healing.

The next step is your preparation.

If you have a reception room, make sure it is warm, with comfortable chairs and maybe some flowers, some soft music playing, some magazines to read, maybe some literature on spiritual healing and possibly a donation box.

It is always very advisable for the healer to sit quietly for say 10 minutes to settle the mind, allow that peace and quiet to be there for you. Sit comfortably, listen to seek attunement with your spirit friends. Once you feel comfortable simply ask your friends to draw close to you, say that you are ready, willing and able to be used as a healing channel and ask to be used by spirit for the healing energy to flow through you to assist all who come to you for help. Sit quietly and send love to your spirit friends. During this quiet time they will be attuning to you, preparing for the work to be done. When you feel ready, thank your spirit friends.

Check your personal cleanliness, your breath and your hands. I favour the healer wearing a white shirt or blouse. I believe it is very important that we healers have a professional approach to healing and our personal etiquette and dress sense can help here. I would not like to see a healer turn up who had not bothered to shave or say had been drinking and smelt of alcohol, or someone who had some of their breakfast down the front of their shirt. Take pride in whatever you do!

When the patient arrives.

Introduce yourself and welcome them, be bright, confident and warm, maybe engaging in some small talk, like the weather, traffic etc.

Show them into your healing room and offer them a seat. Should they have a friend with them, they can be shown into the reception area and asked to wait. Once you are both seated, you should ask the opening question—e.g. "How can I help you?"

Encourage the patient to talk freely and you just listen. What is happening now is that the patient is starting to feel less stressed and becoming more relaxed and comfortable with you. A rapport is building up between patient and healer and you are more aware of what is wrong with the patient. Your spirit guides are also aware of the situation and what action they are organising as regards the healing act.

Fill in your patient's record card, with the assistance of the patient, and explain that all information is confidential and necessary to you the healer.

Once you feel it is time to commence the laying on of hands, it is very necessary that you check with the patient whether or not he or she knows about spiritual healing. You need their permission for you to lay hands on them to facilitate a healing. You need to explain all that is required on their part is for them to relax, sit quietly, close their eyes, and know that you may touch them with your hands lightly. They must be comfortable and feel at ease; encourage them to listen to the music and relax into it. Check their posture, uncross arms and legs, remove glasses if necessary, or heavy top coats etc. At this stage you the healer relax your mind, listen to the music, visualise the healing energy, or maybe a white light entering the patients body and encircling that body. (You as a healer may have some other method or thought pattern you prefer to use—please use what ever you feel comfortable with.) We each of us will over time develop our own personal 'modus operandi'.

You then take up a position behind the patient and mentally express your desire and willingness to be used as a healing channel. You place your hands gently on to the shoulders of the patient and at this stage you say "Thy will be done". You are now handing over control of all healing to your spirit guides.

Please be aware to keep out the 'human element'.

Should you be working using a massage table instead of a chair, the situation would be the same.

When the healing act has been completed, you first give thanks to Spirit for giving their healing energy, and for working with you, and using you as a healing channel. Gently touch the patient on the shoulder and ask them quietly if they are OK. Tell them there is no hurry and that when they are ready they can stand up and gently clench and unclench hands and feet, rubbing hands together. Check how they are feeling for it is possible that the patient may have experienced something that to them was unusual, and they may wish to share this with you before they depart. It is quite likely that this healing session may have stirred something in them that will open them to more spiritual acts or thoughts. Once they are settled, you can work out if a further visit is required, deal with financial arrangements, etc., then escort them to the door, wish them well, and tell them to take care driving. Complete the patient's record card. Obviously, if there is any emotional reaction, etc., after the healing it is advisable for the patient to sit for a while to regain composure before leaving you.

Always make sure that the patient is composed before they leave. Should the patient wish to ask a question, this is a good time to speak with them.

48

Counselling/Communicating/Listening

We use the word 'counselling' in our work, but I believe we should also include 'communicating' and 'listening'.

It has been said that 80% of counselling is listening. This is true, for we healers are there for the patient to have the chance to tell us how they are feeling, and what is happening in their lives. So we sit quietly and listen to what they have to say, without putting our own point of view forward. It is quite possible that we may be the first person who has taken the trouble to listen to them and this in itself will be a big help to them in their healing process. Taking time to listen will also help greatly to build a good rapport between healer and patient and will be of great benefit in the healing act.

Counselling, 'communicating', is an important part of the healing act for it brings the two people concerned together. It is this human contact and interaction between two people that can lead to a successful outcome, in many cases.

Remember also that whilst the two people are together, one listening and one talking, spirit are also very active, playing their part in diagnosing what aspect of their healing abilities will be needed to treat the patient. When the healer initially lays hands on to the patient, Spirit are ready to proceed with the healing in whatever manner they have decided is most suitable for that person.

I would like to stress to you that we as healers, when we talk of counselling, are in no way trying to say we are psychologist or psychiatrists. Of course we are not; we are Healers, first and foremost; 'spiritual healers', whose one desire is to help that person.

Let us look at some suggestions to follow:

1. Counselling or communicating enables us to meet the patient in a friendly environment, a non-threatening situation to them. Remember they may well have been elsewhere and not been treated too well.
2. They may be stressed, in pain, or emotionally upset when they come to you. By simply making them feel welcome and showing empathy and compassion, you help to instil confidence in the patient.
3. They may well be nervous and lacking confidence and seeking re-assurance which the healer, by his or her caring and confident manner, will be able to give them.
4. "A problem shared is a problem halved". How many of you, by being able to talk to someone and tell them your problem, have gained much benefit? Most people don't want to listen to someone with problems—it's human nature. We as healers listen in an attentive manner and simply let them talk it out.
5. To the patient their own problem is a big one and so the healer acts in a non-judgemental way at all times.
6. At all times we seek to build a rapport with the patient, to give them hope, build their confidence and help them to relax their mind. We know that the mind of the healer has to be a clear channel, and so it will help if the patient also has a clearer, more peaceful mind that will in turn assist the healing act.

In today's world more and more people are suffering from what are called psychosomatic problems which surface in emotional, mental, stress-related symptoms. Stress and worry in the mind will more than likely show up in the physical body, for example a skin complaint or rash, etc.

Whatever the problem may be, it is for our spirit guides to diagnose, and they will put into operation whatever healing is needed for the patient.

49

Preparing for Hands on Healing Sessions

Before we actually commence the laying on of hands on to a patient, we must first seek attunement or connection with the healing guides. We humans as the transformer of the energy should seek to attain with our spirit friends the very best channel for the energy to flow through from the transmitter in the Spirit Realm. It is quite natural for we humans to be used as a channel for healing energy to flow through and the act of attunement should also be seen as a quite natural act.

The healer should sit comfortably and allow all the hustle and bustle of the day to become less in the mind, put aside all the cares and worries of the day and go into a meditative state. The playing of relaxing music can also help. We ask the healer to visualise a beach scene, a walk through a lovely garden, any thing that you feel comfortable with and that suits you. Don't try to force things. It should be a natural progression for you. Whilst sitting quietly the healer begins to feel more peaceful, more relaxed. We are sitting to make the connection with our spirit friends and so we ask our spirit guides to draw close to us, we ask for protection and that we may be used as a channel for the healing energy to flow through. We say that we are ready to serve and to be used as a channel, we are ready, willing and able to be used as an instrument by Spirit. Visualise energy as a white light entering our body through our crown chakra.

Again, if you have a method that you feel comfortable with, please use it.

As already stated, the act of attunement is a very natural progression. Do not bring the human element into it. By this I mean that whilst you are sitting quietly, don't start to doubt that your spirit friends are there. Don't wonder if you are doing it right. Don't expect a message from Spirit to say they have arrived. Keep your thoughts and doubts out of it. Remember that we humans have a physical mind which is more concerned with the physical things in life, the daily events and feelings. We also have a spirit mind which is linking with the spirit side of us and it is this which must become ascendant and dominant to facilitate the job at hand, which is transmission of Spirit power and not the mundane, every day thoughts we may have.

The act of fine-tuning is, I believe, done by our spirit guides who, I maintain, have been working with us, preparing us for the work we shall do as healers. I would also suggest that we are unaware of this at the physical level. Nevertheless, it plays a significant part in our development. Because the physical body is of a much more dense material than our other spirit bodies, it is logical that we cannot change our rate of vibration to match that of spirit. Spirit, vibrating at a much higher level, has to reduce their vibrations to enable attunement to take place.

Very simply put, we, as the Healer, sit quietly, say our prayer to God for help and guidance and ask our spirit friends to draw close to us. Express the desire from our hearts and with love to them, that we wish to be of service to Spirit, to be used as a healing channel, and ask that God sends the healing energy through us as the instrument, that we may help to alleviate suffering in the patient.

The patient will already have been advised that we shall be laying our hands on to them and have expressed the fact that they are OK with this contact.

We then stand behind them and place our hands gently on their shoulders. At this moment we ask mentally of our spirit guides to send the healing energy through us from the world of Spirit. A contact has been made with the patient and with spirit. We say "thy will be done," and allow whatever is to happen to happen. Spirit now takes control and all is left to them.

You may work with touching the body with the hands or, as some healers do, keep the hands an inch or so from the body. This is a matter of technique only, as each method works just as well. It is your decision to work in whichever way you feel comfortable.

Next place the hands, when you feel it right, to the side or top of the head. Hold them there until you feel so moved and then place one hand on or near the patient's brow and the other at the nape of the neck or top of the spine.

This is the first method you will use, at the beginning of your healing career. You may also wish to place your hand over each of the chakras. As you pass your hands over the body you may feel sensations like heat, cold, etc.

As you become more experienced you will be able to interpret the significance of these feelings. It doesn't matter at all if you do not feel anything. Remember, we are all different and all work with differing techniques. It is Spirit who is doing the healing and not us.

If a patient tells you that they have a particular problem area, let us say an elbow or knee, we start our healing on the shoulders, head, etc., and then go to the problem area and place our hands on this spot. It is not vitally necessary for us to do this for the energy will be directed where it needs to go. For obvious reasons the patient will be pleased that we did place our hands on the spot and so they are happy. If we do not place our hands on the spot that the patient indicates the problem lies, they may interpret this as ignoring their advice, and it may undermine their confidence in us. So, by virtue of the fact that we want the patient to be comforted and the healing to be successful, we would naturally follow their instructions and place our hands where they have indicated the problem to be. When we feel that the healing has finished, we take our hands gently back to the shoulders and quietly ask the patient if they are feeling OK, and establish that they are 'back with us'.

Most patients can be seen and the healing done by seating the patient on a chair. However, if you are fortunate enough to have a massage table, the patient can lie down on the table and the healing can take place as described above. If, for example, the patient has a back problem they can lie on their front, which enables the healer to work more easily on the problem area. One may still pass hands over the chakras in the same way.

Always make sure that the patient is OK and has come back to earth, so to speak, because some people can be affected (in a nice way) by the increase of energy being absorbed. So be sure they are quite OK and maybe advise them to have a cup of tea before they venture home.

50

A Pictorial Guide

When it comes to the laying on of hands many people are unsure of where they should place their hands on the patient. Should they touch the patient, or should they place their hands near the patient? If near a patient—how near?

I am what I call a touch healer. I feel that by my touching the patient it gives them a sense of comfort and confidence in me, the healer. I know of others who like to place their hands about 8 centimetres from the patient's body. Please remember to keep it simple, use whichever method you feel comfortable with. A combination may suit you best. Always remember that it is Spirit working through you, and so as you progress more into healing, changes in your method may well occur.

"Keep it simple," and you will be successful.

I have put together a set of photographs to give you some guidelines for you to follow as you commence your healing journey.

Procedures to follow.

The first thing that I do when I know someone is coming to see me for healing is to sit quietly to calm my mind. I listen to some nice music of my choice. I sit quietly and simply ask my spirit friends to come close to me and to be with me. I ask them to use me as a channel for healing energy to flow through me, from the world of Spirit, to flow to the patient to help them in which ever way Spirit see fit to do. I say to them that I am ready, willing and able to be used as a channel for healing and leave all healing in their capable hands. I express my love for them, and say God Bless. I then say a short prayer and I am ready to start.

Section 1

Picture 5. We have finished the counselling session with the patient and they understand the need for them to sit comfortably and to relax. Good rapport has been established and they are quite happy for you to lay hands on them.

Take up your position behind the patient and place your hands gently on to their shoulders. As soon as you touch the patient, the link has been made for Spirit to work and they are there and know exactly what needs to be done. At this stage I visualise a rose bud opening slowly to become a full beautiful rose. This symbolises that my channel is open and I now listen to the music and leave all in the hands of my spirit friends. I leave my hands in this position for several minutes before I move to the next position.

Picture 6. Take the hands gently from the shoulders and place them approximately three inches around the head area. This is not putting pressure on the person's head. Again I hold this position for several minutes before we go to the next position.

Picture 7. I take a step to the right and place my right hand near the patient's forehead and my left hand on their neck area. I hold

this position for several minutes before I move on to the next position.

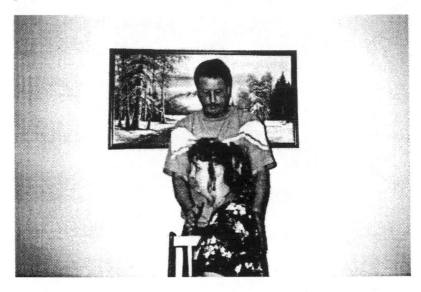

Picture 8. I move my hands down the patient's body, one hand at the front and one at the back. We pass our hands over the chakras as we scan down the patients body. We proceed slowly and go down to the base chakra area and then come back up to the head area. Note in this photograph, the male healer's hand positions, and the right hand approximately 3 to 4 inches away from the female's body, and the left hand touching the body. Common sense prevails here and is following the healer's code of conduct. Retain this procedure for several minutes or for however long you feel inclined. It is quite permissible for the healer to kneel down whilst scanning the body.

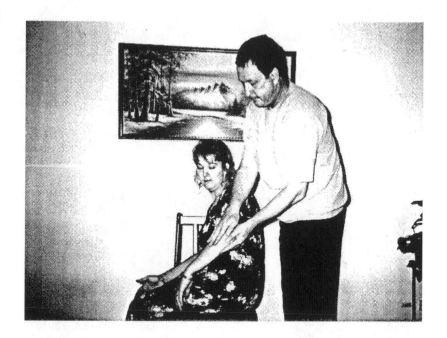

Picture 9. In the case of a specific problem area being advised by the patient (in this case an arm problem) I always complete the prior hand placings before I attend to the specific problem area. Once the procedure has been followed I place my hands on the problem area and hold them in that position for several minutes, to enable healing energy to be passed to the patient. The very fact that my hands are placed on to the patient's area of pain gives them confidence and more peace of mind.

Once we have completed the procedures for hand placement (Pictures 5 to 9) we then place our hands back gently onto the shoulders of the patient and check if they are okay and allow them to sit for a few minutes to adjust.

Once the healing has been completed I thank my spirit friends, and make sure that the patient is all right. I then visualise that lovely rose and see it closing up into a small rose bud. This symbolises that the healing channel is closed. I use this technique of opening and closing at the very start of a healing session and when all healing has taken place for the day. After a healing session it is quite normal for the patient to feel very sleepy and very relaxed. They should not drive home like this, so a cup of tea before they leave is a good idea. If there is an emotional response, some tears, that is quite in order for the patient needs to release and let out some of the emotional feelings they have been keeping inside. Be supportive and tell them that it is all right for them to shed a tear, it's part of the healing process.

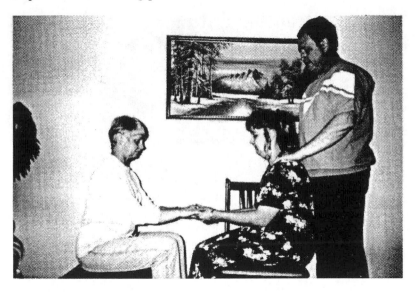

Picture 10. If two people wish to work together as healers I think this is a great idea. One will take the position at the back of the patient and place hands gently on to the patient's shoulders. The other will sit on a chair facing the patient and take their hands. The link has been established and each healer seeks the help of their spirit friends. Healing is now taking place. Note that the patient is sitting side-on to the chair. This is a good idea for it helps the healer to attend to back problems more easily. A stool with no back is an advantage.

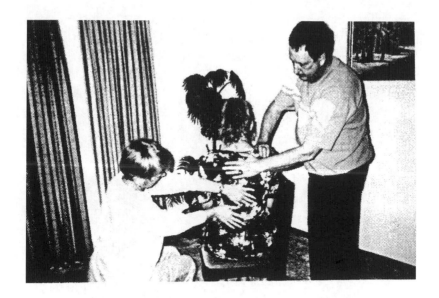

Picture 11. The patient has expressed to the healers that she has a problem with her back. In this situation both healers have placed their hands onto the patient's back area. It is good practise for healers working together to discuss where their hands are to be placed, particularly if one is a probationary healer. Valuable experience and confidence can be gained by working together.

Section 2

One of the great assets of spiritual healing is the very fact that healing can be given using only the humble chair, which is available in every home. It is a simple matter to ask the patient to sit down on a chair and for the healer to then give healing. For groups who hold healing sessions, the fact that really all that is necessary is a chair means that there is very little outlay required. If a healer has to visit a patient in their own home, they don't need to take anything with them.

However, the portable fold-up massage table has been a very useful development for healing therapies. A person is better able to relax when lying down than in the sitting position. The table makes it easier for the healer to access the patient in the horizontal position. I use basically the same hand position for my healing using the massage table.

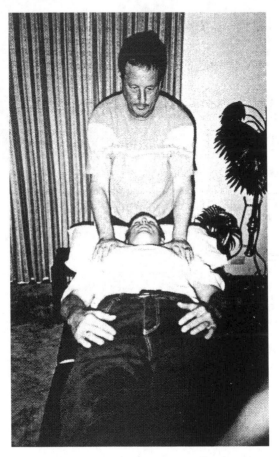

Picture 12. The patient lays on the table with a pillow under the head. The healer takes up a position at the end of the table and places his hands on the shoulders of the patient and holds this position for several minutes. Standing in this position, take the hands from the shoulders and gently place them around the head area, and hold this position for several minutes.

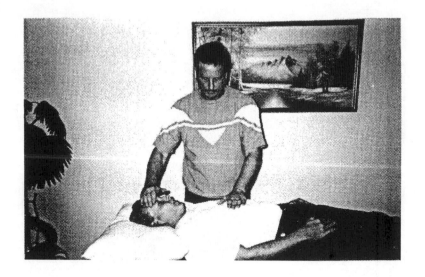

Picture 13. The healer then moves to his left and takes a position with both hands over the chakras. The right hand commences over the head area, whilst the left hand is over the heart area. The healer then moves down the body, each hand being held over a chakra area for a period of time.

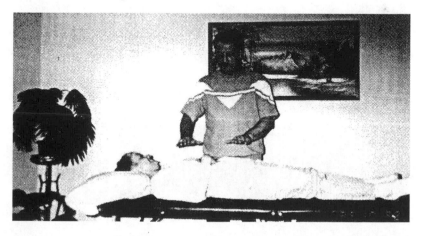

Picture 14. The patient being a lady, note how the healer holds both hands just over the body and Chakras centres, and is not actually touching; again, common sense prevails here (refer Code of Conduct).

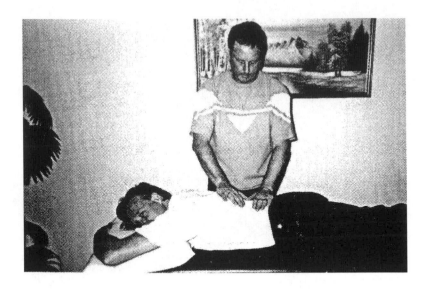

Picture 15. The patient has asked for relief for a back problem. We ask the patient to lay on the tummy so that the back is easily accessible to the healer. The healer can then place his hands over the problem area.

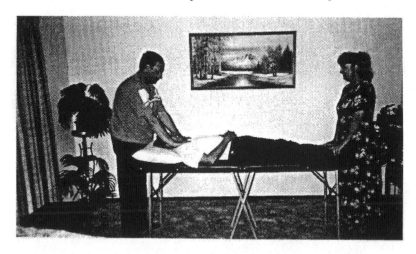

Picture 16. Where two healers wish to work together the procedure is the same. One healer—I call this person the lead healer—takes the position at the head area of the patient, whilst the fellow healer takes a position of holding the feet of the patient.

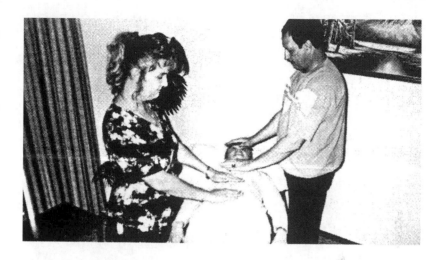

Picture 17. The lead healer moves to his left, places his right hand over the head area, third eye chakra, and his left hand over the heart area chakra. Meanwhile the fellow healer moves to their left and also places a hand over one of the chakras as seen in the picture. In these positions both healers can move up and down the patient quite comfortably without disturbing each other. Proceed slowly to scan the body.

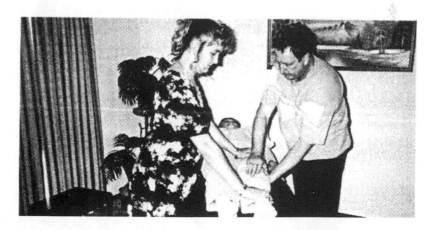

Picture 18. In this picture the patient has mentioned a problem with her left leg. Both healers apply hands to this area. The patient relaxes. Please note that no force or manipulation is used, just a

simple laying on of hands. Once the healing has been completed both healers return to their original starting positions.

Picture 19. When I am working with a probationary healer I always take the position holding the patients hands, (with the patient sitting) or holding the feet, when using a table. This enables me to give healing energy, directed by Spirit. It also allows the probationer to build confidence by actually moving the hands over the patient and helps new healers to gain experience. I firmly believe that the main thing that probationary healers need is confidence. They will only get confidence and become accomplished healers by actually doing the healing. I remember when I was just starting, I met people who had big egos whose idea of teaching was by saying, "Watch me, I will show you what to do." I vowed then I would never follow this path. I get a real thrill out of seeing healers develop.

I should like to emphasise a couple of points regarding the healing methods.

Firstly, to remember that we are all different and you must choose whichever way you feel comfortable with. I have offered some guidelines to help you; take from them what you will.

It is most likely that you the healer will feel heat from your hands when you touch the patient, this is perfectly okay.

Do not be too concerned about when to move your hands to the next position, for as you practise more it will become very natural to you.

Some people feel hot and cold sensations when they scan their hands over the patient.

Some people say that they see colours, or maybe spirit guides; some say that they hear messages. Some healers say that they feel pain when their hands are near a certain area on the patient's body. Some healers believe that they are able to diagnose the problem.

My advice to you is please do not worry what other healers are doing. One does not have to see or hear Spirit to be a wonderful healer. If you do experience any of the other sensations that is fine also, we are all different, all at different levels of healing ability. We all have different spirit guides who use us for healing and we are all on our own individual journey. Please be guided by Spirit, for they are responsible for all healing, and it is they who decide which method to use.

There is no time limit for healing and I would suggest that approximately 15-20 minutes be allowed for the healing act. This allows you to place your hands on to different positions on the patient for approximately 2-3 minutes. Again it will depend on what problems we are dealing with for the patient, and on your level of experience. As you do more healing you will perfect your technique.

"Keep it simple and sincere."

51

Absent or Distance Healing

There are basically two types (if we can call them that) of healing. First we have what we call contact or hands on healing, as described in previous chapters. Then there is absent healing, sometimes also referred to as distant healing, which occurs when the person requiring healing is not present, and in fact may be across the other side of the world.

Absent healing could be described as: "The use of the power of thought to help people get well."

This type of healing is again controlled by our healing friends in Spirit, and the process works along the same lines as contact healing. Distant healing can be performed by a single individual or a group healing session. It is very useful for persons who do not live near a spiritual healer. It can also be used to send healing to a person who, for whatever reason, does not wish to see a healer, or who maybe does not believe in healing. The sending of distant healings can be of help to a healer who is very busy and they can then accomplish a lot of healings by sitting quietly and attuning with Spirit to send the healing thoughts.

The process we use to send distant healing to a person far away is outlined as follows, taking a hypothetical case to illustrate the situation.

You the reader/healer and I are going to do some distant healing. We have been given a photograph of a lady who lives in Los Angeles, USA. The photograph has been given to us by her daughter, asking for healing for her mother. I would seek to obtain brief details about that person; for example, a name, address, city, is the person a relative or a friend, etc. It is not really necessary to know the illness, although most people requesting healing for someone will automatically tell you. We would then take the photograph in our hands and say an opening prayer. We sit quietly and meditate on the picture, we ask Spirit for help. We state to Spirit that we wish to send healing to the said person, and ask them to take charge. We can then visualise a healing ray, going from us in our room to that person in the room where they are. We may visualise the person being enveloped in a lovely white light. If there is a particular way that you like to imagine this healing taking place, then please go with whatever feels good for you. We are mentally asking our own spirit guides to link up with the sick person's guardian angel, to initiate a healing for that person. We are sending out healing thoughts to that person who is in need and the thoughts are sent with love. We ask for Spirit to help that person in whatever way they can. We send our love to our guides and thank them. We then leave the healing in their capable hands.

In closing I like to say a little prayer thanking Spirit for their help.

52

Help in Getting Started

The following notes have been compiled to hopefully be of assistance to those readers who may not have the benefit of a Healing Group as a back up system. Some readers may live in areas where there are healing organisations, and my advice to you is to join such an alliance. There is strength in numbers, and it is by all of us working together that we can advance the practise of spiritual healing.

As noted in an earlier chapter, people living in the United Kingdom have an excellent organisation called the National Federation of Spiritual Healers which is at the forefront in the promotion and practise of Spiritual Healing. The work they have done with the medical profession has, I believe, helped to ensure that the way ahead for spiritual healing is very bright. If you live, as many of us do, in places where spiritual healing is not well known or practised, and where very few healers are working, then we need extra help and faith.

The following ideas are not set out in any sequence, but as they come to mind.

Always remember that your Spirit friends (your 'management') are with you to help and direct you. (Even though at times you may doubt this.)

1. Try to be more patient about your progress "hasten slowly."
2. Try to keep your faith when things get tough.

3. Accept that there will be tests to overcome on the path ahead.
4. If you feel so inclined, read books and attend courses.
5. If it is possible, try to work with trained, experienced healers.
6. Remember the saying, "Only when the pupil is ready can the Teacher arrive." "Only when it is right for you, will it happen for you."
7. Work on your own self-development and spiritual growth.
8. Work on your abilities of listening and communicating with people. (People will be directed to you).
9. As you unfold the aspects of humility, empathy, compassion and desire to be of service, so your healing will become purer and stronger.
10. Be down to earth in your approach to healing.
11. Keep it simple and sincere. (The KISS principle).
12. You are a 'sower of seeds', so remember people will judge you by the way you are living your life.
13. Be open minded to other people's ideas, etc. Maybe try other therapies, to see what you think.
14. Care for your own personal hygiene.
15. Keep your sense of humour—smile, enjoy life.
16. Practise 'absent healing'.
17. Keep a state of balance in your life—moderation is the key.
18. Your spirit friends give much love to you; do what you do also with love.
19. Some meditation and just sitting quietly will help you to develop awareness.

I am sure that you will have some helpful hints that you could add to my list.

53

Death, Dying and Living

Something to think about: All of us at some time or another have lost a loved one. A close relative, a friend, somebody we love and who has loved us, has gone from our lives on this earthly plane. When this happens, under whatever circumstances, however young or old the person was, have you ever asked yourself, "Will we meet again?"

We attend a funeral parlour, prior to the burial or cremation, and we see our loved one for the last time, the physical body resting so serene and still in the coffin. Have you ever thought to yourself, "Here lies someone who I loved and who loved me; love was there for many years. A closeness, a bond, something that words cannot describe. All that we shared, the love given and received over many years. Can this really be the end?"

We know that "Love is never wasted, for if it does not benefit the receiver: it benefits the giver." Would God, who has created a perfect world in which we live and whose teaching is 'Love' and in whose image we were made, have made a mistake? Jesus the Christ preached 'Love' during his short life on earth; He taught us that anything is possible providing 'Love' is with us.

Why is it that we are seemingly brought up to fear death? There is definitely a lack of spiritual teaching about death. We need not fear it, we need to understand it. As one door closes, so another opens. Let us try to look at the situation calmly and logically, and think about it. There would be absolutely no point or purpose in our living if there was not a continuation or something after this earthly life. It doesn't make sense for it to just end here, does it?

Would God, whose teachings all centre around love, bring us together to love and be loved and then just end it and separate father from daughter, mother from son, forever? I think not—for I know this is not so.

"Love never dies—it is the strongest force in the Universe." We shall meet again, we and our loved ones, who have gone from us temporarily.

So take heart and know that we shall all meet again. I don't know where or when. It is part of our spiritual progress and destiny.

54

Medical—Scientific—Spiritual

Until doctors accept that they must begin to treat the individual as body, mind and spirit, and not just the physical sickness; until they embrace a more wholistic approach, learn to care for not only the physical body but the mind and the spirit also, it is unlikely that we shall achieve true happiness, health, contentment, and a better world for us all. For too long now we have seen medicine concentrate far too much attention on the healing of the physical body. Far too much emphasis is being placed on drugs, antibiotics, and whilst there have been some wonderfully beneficial advances which have helped mankind, we have also seen a great reliance on drugs prescribed for just about every thing under the sun. It is because of this over use of drugs that I believe more and more people are turning away from orthodox medicine and changing to what is termed alternative medicine. Of course some of these alternatives can lead to abuse in the wrong hands. There needs to be some form of government regulation or control over such therapies, which would be acceptable to the medical profession. It must surely be beneficial to all of us if the medical profession were able to accept the credentials of some of these other methods of healing and maybe incorporate them into their practise. We could then see a turning towards a more wholistic method of treating body, mind and spirit.

The 1958 Report on Spiritual Healing by the Church of Scotland, quotes thus: "In any consideration of the relationship between scientific medicine and spiritual or divine healing, two facts must be clearly recognised."

A) All healing is ultimately of God, who alone is the source of life and well being. Those who combat and overcome sickness and disease are agents whom God chooses.

B) It is a mistake for spiritual healing to be thought of as a substitute for medical treatment, or as a final resort to be used only when medical treatment appears to have failed. They are to be thought of rather as two different, complementary methods of dealing with disease, and in many cases of illness both may be required if the patient is to obtain complete health. It is to be hoped that we do see, in the none too distant future, all healing methods working together for the sake of mankind.

55

Playing our Part

Many people, who start to become involved in spiritual healing, have likely been told that they have 'healing ability'. To some this can be a big 'ego trip'. To others, not knowing very much about healing, it can be quite a novelty and an intriguing subject to delve into. They believe that the way to go is to attend a course, do some meditation, read books on the subject, and start to lay hands on to people. They think that this alone will develop the divinely bestowed ability of spiritual healing. Some good work may take place, and some people may be helped, but far more could be achieved if we are prepared to work on ourselves.

We are but a channel for Spirit to use, and to play our part we must, 'perfect the instrument'. I have found that most of the healers I have met have not had an 'easy life'. They have experienced many set backs, heartaches, struggles and tests in their life. They have come through and learnt from experiences, and this has helped to develop their humility and empathy. Any growth that takes place may not always be a pleasant experience, for it usually involves radical changes taking place in our lives.

I believe Spirit are testing us, 'perfecting their instrument', and it is my strong belief that Spirit start from very early on to develop us, and to make subtle changes in our emotional, spiritual and psychic levels. It is as if we are being, how can I say it, 'tuned up', rather like a master violinist would tune his violin. I am sure that we are guided, directed and manoeuvred by them, so that we are on track, meeting people we need to meet, being in places we need to be. For some the process may be quicker than for others, for we all have free will, and may stray off the path.

If Spirit (our healing guides) are patiently doing their part, how can we do our part?

I do not believe that it is an easy task, nor do I have the answer in 'three easy lessons'. Living in a very materialistic society with little thought to the spiritual side of life makes it extremely hard for us to live our lives in a spiritual way. That is not to say that we cannot strive to be spiritual in the way we each relate to one another.

56

We Need to Work on Ourselves

A) *On our emotion and feeling:* To understand and accept our feelings, and to overcome such sensations as hate, fear, envy, jealousy, etc.

B) *On our thought and worries:* To understand and accept we are humans, who worry about all manner of things. We may be aware that worrying about something doesn't help; yet we still do it. What we think, if it is negative, can also be harmful.

C) *On our actions, and other motives:* To understand and accept why we are doing things. What are our motives? Are our actions done in a Spiritual way, is our motive a spiritual one? Do things because you really want to do them, and not because you feel you have to.

D) *Needs as against wants:* To understand and accept that there is a big difference between what we need and what we want. "Is it not said that the less desires a person has, the happier they will be?"

E) *The guilt trip:* To understand and accept that if we have done our best, we do not need ever feel guilty. We are not responsible for any body else's life but our own.

F) *Humility:* To understand and accept that the gift of healing is divinely bestowed. A wonderful ability, to be used to help mankind. Accept it with humility and develop it to the best of your ability.

If we are worried, emotionally upset or feeling guilty about something, then we cannot act as a clear channel for Spirit to use.

Many people search for knowledge from books, courses etc., but that will only take you to a certain level of ability

It is only when we work on ourselves, and have love in our hearts, when we can feel that love and give that love freely, that we can perform to the best of our ability. Only then can Spirit use us as an instrument for healing and obtain the best results.

The patience and caring shown to us by our spirit friends, and the great love that they have for us, is wonderful and it is always there for us to receive. We only have to ask.

When we love it is the heart that judges and not the head. Simply LOVE Simply.

Many people's concept of love is often experienced as a sentimental emotion, like 'romantic love' as depicted in novels. Some people may never progress any further than this stage, which is sad because they are not developing spiritually. Also, a great number of men are not able to express their feelings, for they see it as a weakness, when in actual fact understanding and showing our emotions is a sign of strength.

We can look at love as being a reciprocal act: we are loved, so we in turn give love. In many people's eyes, love is associated with sex. If we could aspire to the highest form of love it would be on a different level, far more emotional than we can experience on the physical level.

The goal should be an unconditional love, in which nothing is sought in return. A big ask for we mortals in this material world.

57

"Sceptical stroke patient praises spirit healing."

An article from the UK newspaper, *Psychic News,* September 15, 1990.

> An Australian spiritual healer said last week he would like to see practitioners working in hospitals 'down under' enjoying the same privileges as their British counterparts.

> David Clements of the Perth Healing Sanctuary was interviewed by local journalist Lynn Robbins.

> Ms Robbins wrote that as research and technology struggle to maintain pace with the constantly manifesting health issues, a demand for a much greater knowledge about natural remedies and alternative healing has emerged.

> Orthodox medicine has, in the main, concentrated on physical symptoms.

> However, it is becoming increasingly recognised, not least by doctors, that curing the symptoms often does not mean curing the cause.

Man is a complicated creature. He has a mind and a spirit as well as a body. Unless all three elements are working together in harmony, illness results.

The journalist explained that healers aimed to link sufferers with invisible forces or energies to produce harmony.

David, a National Federation of Spiritual Healers member, said it was important to realise that spiritual healing and orthodox medical practise are not in competition with each other.

In England, spiritual healers work not only with individual medical practitioners but also within the hospital environment, he said. We would like to see a similar situation developing here.

Ms Robbins said that there was no mystery to spiritual healing. It is not magic, but a spiritual science known and accepted in may parts of the world.

When being treated, the healer helps the patient to relax mentally and physically, and then allows the healing energy to flow through by placing his or her hands on or near the recipient.

Patients may experience a flow of energies with feelings of warmth, cooling, tingling or relaxation. There are no side effects, only benefits.

The journalist spoke to patient Mervyn Wilson, 54, who last year suffered two strokes within three weeks.

He left hospital in a wheel chair, with restricted arm movement and could walk only in an extremely limited way and needed help in dressing.

Mr Wilson became very depressed. Whilst very sceptical about healing, at his wife's insistence he visited David's sanctuary.

"It was the best decision I could have made, "he said. "My walking has improved, and I have some arm movement."

I can now manage stairs, walk over beach sand, and am currently playing indoor bowls regularly.

David Clements is very professional and has a genuine belief in his healing. This generates confidence in his patients.

David gave me hope and motivation where I previously had none. My condition has improved, physically and mentally. I now enjoy a positive outlook.

Subsequently his specialist commented: I don't know what you are doing, but keep it up! It's working.

Ms Robbins said it was important to stress that patients should continue medical treatment in conjunction with spirit healing.

There was no doubt in Mr Wilson's mind that healing has assisted him in making major improvement in his condition. His physiotherapist has commented on his excellent progress.

The Perth Healing Sanctuary has also successfully treated patients with asthma, food allergies, arthritis, depression and allied problems.

The sanctuary is not concerned with distinctions of race, class or religious belief, said David.

Everyone is welcome. There are many people out there who can benefit physically, emotionally and mentally through spiritual healing.

Our future goal is to establish a permanent full time sanctuary to give those people the opportunity to seek help at any time.

58

Questions and Answers Section

During the time I have been conducting courses on spiritual healing, many questions have been asked by those participating. Many people when they want to ask questions say, "It's probably a dumb question, but!"

Let me say this—I don't believe there are any dumb questions. We are all searching, and a great way to gain knowledge is to ask questions of a person who has knowledge and wisdom. It should always follow that the answers given should be acceptable to the questioner. If it appeals to your common sense and gives that inner emotion or intuition of 'a good feeling', then I believe that this, your guidance system, is telling you that it is OK.

Men have what we call 'gut feelings', about people, places, situations, whilst women have that wonderful 'women's intuition'. How many times have you had that feeling, that something just 'doesn't feel right', yet gone against it, and later on landed in trouble. So people, learn to trust that feeling, because I believe that it is your spirit guardian advising you. For as you may not hear them if they spoke to you, they transmit it to you in another way.

The questions are in no order preference, and I have endeavoured to answer them as best I can. As is my usual approach, I shall try to do this in an as easily understood a way as I can.

QUESTION: I don't really understand why I am here at the course. I don't know much about healing, but have had some sort of inner feeling, which I can't seem to accept. But when by chance I picked up the article on your course, I felt I should attend.

ANSWER: You say 'by chance', my friend. My understanding of how Spirit work leads me to say that there are 'no coincidences'. Not by chance did you receive the article. I believe you were guided by Spirit, so it would seem that the time is now right for you to take the next step. For remember "A journey of a thousand miles begins with the first step". Good luck!

QUESTION: I am a social drinker and a smoker and I enjoy both. Will this inhibit my healing ability?

ANSWER: I believe there has to be balance in life, and a sense of moderation. I see nothing wrong in having a glass of wine and the occasional cigarette: you enjoy them, and it gives you a nice feeling; if you were made to stop, it would make you feel uneasy and cause you to be unbalanced. Providing you don't drink or smoke too much, and do keep it in moderation, I feel an occasional smoke or drink can be quite OK. We must always try to care for our body, which is the temple of the Spirit. Keep your drinking and smoking in moderation and most definitely away from the healing sessions.

QUESTION: I have difficulty with using the word God as the source of the healing energies. I don't know why, it just doesn't sit right with me.

ANSWER: That is OK, we humans cannot explain who, where or what God is, it is beyond our comprehension. I would ask you what you could accept. The Red Indians of America were very close to nature and very spiritual people. They prayed to 'The Great White Spirit'. Some people say 'The Absolute', 'A Cosmic Force', 'Universal Intelligence', 'The All Powerful'. It comes down to you and what you feel comfortable with, because really, it's all one and the same. So go by what you feel comfortable with.

QUESTION: I don't like the use of the word God because it suggests that God is a man, and being a woman, I can't go along with this.

ANSWER: I believe the previous question and answer cover this situation. I personally don't believe that God is either male or female. I believe we also as a spirit are neither male nor female, but can be both. If we look at reincarnation, we don't come back as only a man or only a woman each time, do we? So I believe the Spirit is above this gender question. I suggest you use whatever is comfortable for you personally; if you want to see God as a woman, I'm sure God won't mind.

QUESTION: I have a friend who doesn't believe in spiritual healing and thinks it's bunkum. Could they be healed even if they don't have any faith in it?

ANSWER: It is more conducive to healing taking place if the person has an open mind to it. But don't let it upset you, for when we lay our hands on to the patient we say "Thy will be done," and so pass the decision as to whatever is going to take place on to our spirit guides. It is they who are doing the healing and not us, and so whatever happens is up to them.

It is a known fact that many people who do have a great faith in healing and the healer seem not to receive the miracle cure they desire, yet sometimes a non-believer seems to. As all is known by Spirit; there is a reason for everything that takes place. As long as we trust and have faith in them, we have played our part in the healing act. I believe every healing given does help the patient in some way. Nobody goes away without some help being given to them.

QUESTION: I am now 63 years old and retired. I have had an interest in these sort of things, like healing, but I think I'm too old to get involved, especially as I look at all the younger people here on the course.

ANSWER: Please don't let that stop you. One of the great things about this work is that age is no barrier. You could be 90 years old and still be a wonderful healer or medium. As you have now retired, I'm sure you have more time to devote and will be able to become more involved. Keep going, OK?

QUESTION: Since we have been doing the hands on healing and hearing people's comments, it seems that other people are seeing and hearing things and I don't. Does that mean I am not as capable of Healing as they are?

ANSWER: No, not at all. We must always remember that we all are different and that we work in a different manner with our healing guides. Some people do see, some people do hear and some people feel energies where the problem may be. I don't believe it really matters, for haven't we learnt that it is not us humans, but Spirit that controls every aspect of the healing act. Trust your spirit guide and know that if you are meant to see or hear, then it will happen, in their time not yours. Please read the chapter on "The Human Element" which will answer your question in more depth. Remember, *"Only when the pupil is ready—will the teacher arrive."*

QUESTION: I find that when I stand for a long time when I am doing the healing, I have aches in my legs; is it necessary to stand?

ANSWER: No, it isn't necessary to stand. Please make yourself comfortable and have a seat handy. It is quite OK to be seated when you are healing. Remember also to wear shoes and clothes in which you feel comfortable working.

QUESTION: One of my friends who does spiritual healing says that when she passes her hands over the body that she can pick up where the problem is. I don't have this, so does it mean I am not doing healing properly? I just feel a bit inferior with my healing.

ANSWER: Some Healers do possess this ability and work in this way, but a great many healers don't. So you are not alone in this aspect. The big problem can be that some people get carried away with things and the conscious mind and ego come to the fore. The Code of Conduct specifies most strongly that we healers "Do Not Diagnose", so we must tread very carefully on this subject. I have covered this query in the chapter on the "Human Element". I wouldn't let it worry you; keep on doing your healing the way you feel comfortable with, and feel confident that it will all work out for you and you will get the results you seek as you develop more. Just do the work. Leave all to Spirit to organise.

QUESTION: When I see people doing healing, some touch the patient and some hold their hands close to the patient; which is the right way?

ANSWER: I don't believe there is a right or wrong way. I myself believe it is best to touch, as it somehow seems to assure the patient that there is a bonding, and to me appears to strengthen the healing. I believe that in today's society we don't have enough touching.

Touching seems to convey warmth and caring from the one person to the other. I mean, when we meet and greet someone and put our arms around them and hug them, we do touch, don't we? We don't put our arms around them and keep them from touching the other person. I believe it is a matter of technique so please do whichever method you feel comfortable with. I am sure that Spirit can pass the energy through whether you touch or not. I just believe touching is a more personal approach to the healing.

QUESTION: Why is it that far more women than men are involved in spiritual healing? Is there a reason?

ANSWER: Yes, it is a fact that there are far more women than men in not only healing, but other aspects of Spirit, like mediumship, massage, aromatherapy and other therapies. I believe it is so because women are, shall we say, emotional beings; much more aware of emotions, empathy and compassion, and tend to be carers. Men, on the other hand, tend to have a big ego, want to appear as Macho, mustn't show feelings, etc., and in many cases have quite closed minds to many things. Obviously my comments are general, but it would be interesting to see a survey done on the subject. Let me say that it is pleasing to see more men becoming involved, particularly amongst the younger ones.

QUESTION: Both my husband and myself are very keen and interested in spiritual healing and would like to work together. Is this a good idea or not?

ANSWER: I think it's a wonderful idea, good on you. I believe that more people are combining and now working together as healers. As a probationary healer you gain much confidence and knowledge working with an accomplished healer. The other good point is that you can also work singly if the situation calls for it. For example if a woman client comes along she may only wish to see a woman, or reverse the situation, a man comes to you who would prefer to see a man. You are quite adaptable.

It is good to see two people working together and helping each other and those who are in need of healing.

QUESTION: I have read quite a lot of books on healing and many tend to be too technical and hard to understand. They also differ in many cases on their content. Why

ANSWER: There are many books now on healing and yes, I believe some are too technical. I feel many of these books are written by theorists and not by people actually doing hands on healing. Remember also, any book you read is only that person's opinion, and what they believe. It is for you to decide which you feel is right for you. Sadly, today it seems the more mystical and technical we can make healing seem, the more money can be charged. Spiritual healing is, and always has been, a very basic and uncomplicated matter of laying on of hands.

QUESTION: There seem to be quite a few people who advertise that they are healers, using exotic names for their type of healing. They also say things like "using Universal Energy". Their charges are also quite high. What is your opinion on this situation?

ANSWER: Unfortunately there are many people who prey on the vulnerable people in our society. Because many people are searching, they can easily be misled by a person with the wrong motives. We call our healing 'spiritual healing' using energy directed by spirit helpers. These people do not use the word spiritual because it is most definitely not 'Commercial'. We say that people who have the gift of healing have a God given gift. They say that they can, for a huge fee, teach a human being to become a healer. Then you pay more money to become more advanced in healing. I feel that their motives are money orientated in many cases. On earth we are all pupils, learning all the time. All healing comes from God, from Spirit, and Spirit healing energies cannot be directed by humans, only by Spirit—let us be sure on that fact. Some of these people may be being used by Spirit and not be aware of the fact that they have the gift of healing and do not need to pay lots of money to do something they have been given by God.

"What's in a name? A rose by any other name would smell as sweet."

QUESTION: When we attend a healing course we are told that spiritual healing is a very simple matter of laying on of hands. If so, why do we get taught a lot of other things that seem not important?

ANSWER: A good question, which would take me a lot longer to answer properly than I can at present. But let me try to help you to understand. Firstly, you are only just starting to become involved in spiritual healing, and as you go further in to it you will realise that the things you now call irrelevant are useful to know. Many people who come to you as a healer will be searching and want to know more about it—if you cannot tell them, you will lose your credibility.

Also, if you did not have more knowledge about the subject, how could you help probationers to develop? If you are talking to people in the medical profession, it is very handy to have as much knowledge as you can. You may be guided to be a teacher, or in a position of authority; then you will need as much knowledge as you can get.

QUESTION: People tend to use the words "Alternative and Complementary Therapies". Please explain this to us.

ANSWER: Yes, this can be confusing, because they are talking about the same thing. Some people call any therapy which is not supplied by your doctor or general practitioner, alternative. By the same token some people call it 'complementary'. As spiritual healers we wish to work with the medical profession, and we much prefer the use of the word complementary when describing our healing. I feel also that the word "alternative" can be intimidating to some in the medical profession. Complementary suggests that we healers can work in conjunction with doctors (as indeed some healers are already doing). Alternative may suggest to a doctor that the therapy could be seen as a substitute to that which the doctor practices.

In the future I believe that healers and medical doctors will work closer together.

QUESTION: My Husband tends to ridicule and run down my interest in spiritual healing.

ANSWER: This seems to be quite a common occurrence, mainly on the part of men. It could quite possibly be a case of insecurity on his behalf. A fear of losing you and your attention, and possibly a fear of the unknown. Remember there is nothing in life to be feared, but to be understood. Don't push him, and try to make him accept your ideas; rather, take it slowly and let him find out when he is ready to do so.

"Knowledge advances slowly by steps, and not by leaps".

QUESTION: Is it wrong to charge for healing? Several people have said to me that healing is a gift and so you shouldn't charge for it. Can you advise me?

ANSWER: The question of whether one should charge money for healing is always being argued about, and there really is no answer that would be acceptable to all parties concerned. But let me try to help you here. The decision is a personal one! It is up to the individual person to determine his or her choice of whether to charge or not. On the subject of healing being a gift, well I believe that clairvoyance and clairaudience are also gifts. But you don't see many clairvoyants doing free readings, do you? Some people adamantly refuse to charge for healing; if that is their wish, that's fine. Some people ask for a donation for healing; if that is their wish, that's fine for them. Some people have a nominal charge for healing; that is also fine. I believe that Jesus once said, something like "The servant is worthy of his labour". It really depends on the circumstances; if you have to pay for things like rental of a room, electricity, tea and coffee, etc., the money has to be forthcoming. I myself have done many free healings, have also worked on a donation system, and I have made a charge for healing. Look at another angle to this question, Massage, Reflexology, Reiki, Aroma therapy etc. all charge for the service. If you do decide to have a fee, please make it a reasonable one. Again we go back to the start. It's your choice!

QUESTION: Is it necessary to join a group if one wishes to practise healing? I feel I am a bit of a loner.

ANSWER: No it is not necessary to join a group but I feel that there can be advantages in belonging to a healing group. Contact and communication with others involved in healing can be rewarding, and it can provide good 'back up' for you. If you do go to group meetings, I believe your intuition will let you know if that group is for you.

QUESTION: I have been asked to speak at local mothers meetings on spiritual healing. As I am only quite newly into healing, is this OK?

ANSWER: By all means! I am sure that you will be surprised at the interest shown to you. Give them the opportunity to ask questions, and if possible give willing subjects some hands on healing. Be aware not to preach to them; be natural, and be yourself.

QUESTION: I have a friend who is also involved in healing. She is always telling me how successful the healings are. Now she says she is working in the etheric level, what do you think?

ANSWER: I feel she has much to learn. I believe that a healer who is properly trained and has the right motives has no need to blow their own trumpet. A true healer goes about their business quietly and confidently. It is said self-praise is no recommendation. As for her etheric level quote, does she not understand that all healing is controlled and ordered by Spirit. Whichever level or technique is required will be organised by Spirit and not by her.

QUESTION: Some of my friends and I are very interested in spiritual healing and really want to develop our abilities as quickly as we can. How can we speed things up?

ANSWER: Firstly let me say that it is always nice to meet people who are interested in spiritual healing. The fact is that you cannot speed things up. You cannot make things happen any quicker than they are meant to. Your spirit guides have everything under control; they are very aware of your progress to date. They will know how keen you are to develop and will be pleased about that. Try to have patience, try to take each day as it comes and above all, have faith in your spirit friends. Just allow things to happen as they will when it is right for you.

QUESTION: As a healer I have had patients who want to give me something, but as I do not charge a fee it causes an awkward situation. What should I do?

ANSWER: I do understand, so try to look at the situation in this way. We must be able to receive, as well as to give. For if we cannot receive we deprive someone else of the joy of giving. It need not be money that they give, it could be a bunch of flowers. Think about it.

QUESTION: I have been involved in healing for some time now and want to do more work. It doesn't seem to happen quickly enough. How can I speed it up?

ANSWER: You can't. I understand how you feel, but we must always try to learn patience. Please believe that until it is ready for you, then it won't happen.

Try to have faith and patience.

"Only when the pupil is ready can the teacher arrive."

QUESTION: When we have listened to some people discussing healing, they talk about 'opening' and 'closing'. Seemingly this is a precaution against the healer having any unusual experiences. This worries me, could you help here?

ANSWER: The terms opening and closing refer to the healer being open for Spirit to use as a healing channel. Closing means that the healer has finished the healing for the day and is closing the channel. Every aspect of healing is controlled by our healing friends in the spirit world. They know when a person will arrive, what the problem is and how to solve it. Before I attempt a healing session I always sit quietly and say a prayer and ask for guidance and protection. At the finish of a healing session I always sit quietly and say a prayer, thanking my Spirit friends for their using me as a healing channel. Please do not have fear, for your Spirit friend loves you very much and would not let any harm come to you. Trust in their guidance and allow them to use you as a healing channel and you will be looked after and kept safe. To illustrate it further, it's like you are going to work! You open the shop for business, you do the job, and you then close the shop for business and go home. Please rest assured you will be looked after. Spirit are in control of all situations.

A simple way of opening is to visualise a rose bud gradually opening up to a full flower. Do this before you commence your healing. After you have finished healing for the day you can visualise that flower closing down to become a rose bud once again. This may be of help to you.

59

Reassurance for the Journey

When we take the first steps on the path of our journey into spiritual healing we are embarking on a mission that will help us to fulfil our spiritual evolution. We will not know where this journey will take us, nor who we may meet along the way, but be assured that it will be an adventure, exciting and event filled. There will be times when you will sink to the depths of despair and will feel like giving it all up and forgetting about becoming a healer. Often you will feel alone, not knowing what to do, or which direction to take. On other occasions you may feel that your healing ability is not working, for you don't seem to be seeing many patients.

You may become angry at your spirit friends, for you feel that they have deserted you. Your patience will be tried, time and again, and temptations placed in your path.

There is a reason behind all these occurrences in your life. You are being tested by your spirit guides to see if you really do desire to become a healer; is it from your heart, or just because it strokes your ego. Your guides will check you out, but you cannot fool them for they know what is in your heart. Many exciting episodes will have happened to you on your journey, which will have lifted your spirits and helped you keep going. We need to experience both good and bad, and we cannot get this valuable knowledge from a book. But take heart in knowing that your spirit guides were walking every step of the way with you, guiding and sustaining you. They know that you had to undergo and to pass the many tests they set for you, for only through suffering can emerge the strongest souls.

You are being prepared for the work ahead and all you have experienced and learnt will be of great help in your healing work to come.

The saying "only when the pupil is ready can the teacher arrive" is to my mind the truest statement that can be made. For us healers it means that only when situations in our life are stabilised and we are feeling good about life and are happy and contented with ourselves are we ready to begin the work in earnest.

There will be many times in our life that we will believe that we are ready, for we are impatient and eager to begin. Only our spirit guides are able to make this decision for they are so much wiser than we humans. It is not until they are satisfied that opportunities start to open up for us. If you are not ready to receive knowledge then you will not obtain it.

Look back on your life; do you not feel that you have been guided? People you have met, books that you have read, or places you have visited—nothing has been by chance, all has been according to a plan. The very fact that you have this inner urge to be of service and to heal. It is a calling that has always been with you, a desire to work for the betterment of mankind. This is the spiritual purpose which you chose for this life on earth. Your spirit guides will be behind you all the time to assist and direct you. The experiences that I have lived through during my spiritual journey have given me a clearer understanding of how we are helped by our spirit guides. They are fully aware of the difficulties that people trying to live a spiritual way of life here on earth are facing. In a world in which money, possessions and power are worshipped, where greed and corruption are much to the fore. They understand, for they also have lived on earth at some time during their journey.

I would like to share with you some of the advice that my spirit friends have given to me. It is in the main common sense, and I am sure you all can say "Oh yes, I know that". The problem is that we may be aware of it but we do not put it into practice. They have never preached to me or told me how to run my life. My right of free will is always accepted. It never ceases to amaze me that even when I have my own fixed ideas of how something should be done or how it will all work out, it never evolves the way I think it should. The end result is that whatever situation occurs, it always ends up being done the right way—their way! I am sure many readers will attest to this.

I know it is hard for us to let go and let God take over. Try to just accept and go with the flow. Have patience and trust more in your guides and keep your strong belief for you know what you are doing is right. Enjoy life, live each day as it comes, and stop worrying about the future and let the past go.

What has happened cannot be changed, so learn from it and look forward to the future with confidence. Keep focused on your own life; don't concern yourself with what others are doing. Do not be upset if someone else seems to be advancing quicker than you. Remember we are all on our own personal journey; we are all different. You are at the right stage in your development. You cannot make things happen, no matter how hard you try. Make life easier for yourself by just getting on with living life to the full.

To be judgemental of others is something most of us have at some time or other been guilty of, I know I have. I was angry when I saw people abusing their spiritual or psychic abilities to make money, or ever worse, to give that person false hope. I said to my guide, "Why don't you stop this taking place?"

He replied in a very calm voice, "Son, you can't kill all your enemies. Do what you do, and do it well. Then people will know a good healer from a bad one." I learnt a good lesson from this.

I hope the journey you are taking will be a long and interesting one. I can assure you that your spirit guides will never let you down. They have unbelievable patience and they love you so much. Just get on with your everyday life and you will be amazed, as I have been, how it somehow works out for you, in ways that you least expect. Do not worry if you make mistakes, and sometimes lose faith. Your guides are not judging you, for they love you and will gently pick you up when you fall, always there to support you as you journey on.

Be aware that your spirit guides are also on their journey of development, so each of you in turn is helping the other. As you both travel along on the journey together.

60

Kirlian Photography—Its Origin

What we can now call Kirlian photography was discovered quite by chance. Semyon Kirlian was an electrical and mechanical engineer who lived with his wife Valentina at Krasnodor in the Ukraine. It was whilst he was working on a piece of apparatus that he noticed what we can call electrical activity, between his hand and an electrode. Because this aroused his curiosity he decided to spend time studying the phenomenon. This all started in 1939, and the Kirlians worked on experiments and study for the next 20 years. The Soviet Government classified this work as secret, and so it wasn't until around 1960 that any articles on the subject were allowed to be released. Probably the most well known of the Kirlian experiments was called 'the Phantom Leaf Effect'. The leaf from a healthy plant was photographed. A portion of the leaf was then "cut off", and another picture was taken. The resulting photograph still showed an energy pattern, as if the leaf were a whole one. A great deal of money has been spent by Eastern Block countries in researching the Kirlian process. We in the western world have a lot of catching up to do in this area. There needs to be much more research done before we can utilise and understand how this picturing of energies in the body can be put to beneficial use by doctors and other therapists in our society. I only intend to give a very brief summary on this subject, but there are many good books now available, which will go in to more detail on the subject.

Kirlian photography can also be used to show that energy patterns exist around other things as well as the hands and feet of humans. Picture 31 on page 181 shows the energy patterns around a silver ring that I have worn for many years. We used the same Kirlian process to photograph the ring as used for the hands.

61

Kirlian Photography
A Support for Healing

I am aware that many people who read this book may not know what Kirlian photography is, or how it works, and the results that are obtained by the Kirlian process. Not to worry, I was myself in exactly that position when I first heard about Kirlian photography. I feel I should explain how I became involved. As a Healer I was always trying to be open to other ideas, therapies and methods of healing. I had read books, which made a mention of the Kirlian photography process. But they weren't able to offer very much information. Being aware that the United Kingdom seemed to be the source of many new and innovative ideas, I wrote to my friend Shirley, who I had met during my earlier visit to London.

Shirley Brooker was the chairperson of the National Federation of Spiritual Healers and a very knowledgeable and dedicated lady. Shirley was able to put me in touch with a man called Guy Mason who actually makes Kirlian cameras and lives in Petersfield, Hampshire, not far from London. Correspondence went back and forth between Guy and myself, letters and phone calls galore. Eventually Guy suggested that to really get more information and experience of Kirlian photography I needed to be in England, and to work with Guy, actually using the machine.

I decided to follow his advice and organised my trip to England. Just prior to my leaving Perth to fly to London, I was involved in a car accident, which really should have postponed my trip. I was told I should rest, but being the proverbial slow learner and stubborn also, I didn't take the advice and proceeded on my trip.

I spent a very interesting 3 weeks with Guy and his associate June Yates, using the Kirlian machine in many aspects of the work, and gained much knowledge of how the camera works and how to interpret the pictures that are developed. Guy and June are both very involved in spiritual healing and this further enhanced our work with the Kirlian camera. Guy emphasised that Kirlian photography was very much in its infancy in England, and that we had much to learn about the subject. They both accentuated the need to do the hands on work, taking pictures and discussing those pictures with the client. By doing this it gives you invaluable experience of actually doing the work, using intuition and feelings. In other words "The more you do the better you get".

I am including here some pictures and an interpretation of them. I hope that this will be easier for you to understand what it can do. I believe that Kirlian photography can be of great significance in actually showing the patient their energy levels at that point in time, when they come to you for healing. If we take another picture after the patient has received healing treatment, we should notice an increase in energies (this could apply after one session, or you may wish to apply healing over a period of time). Pictures could be taken before and after therapy. This would establish if the particular therapy used was serving the patient well. The very fact that the patient can actually see for themselves a change must surely assist in the healing process. It would also be beneficial to the healer.

The day may come when orthodox and complementary medicines will use a Kirlian type camera to assist them in their healing work.

Technology is developing at a very fast rate and I am sure that new developments in the field of measuring energies will produce much more sophisticated machines than we now have at our disposal. Naturally much more research has to be done before we are able to fully utilise a Kirlian type camera to identify sickness.

62

What is Kirlian Photography?

It may also be referred to as electro-imaging, electrography, or corona photography.

"A witness to the meeting of mind, body and Spirit"

Kirlian photography is a method of picturing the energy field around both living and man made things. We are primarily using it to picture the energy patterns around a person's hand, forming part of their personal aura. These are unique to each individual, and continually changing in response to activity and health. They are influenced by the state of the Mind, Body and Spirit. The pictures taken can give an experienced practitioner an indication of the balance of personality, emotions and lifestyle, and can reveal such psychic or spiritual abilities as healing ability and mediumship.

Kirlian photography could be invaluable in establishing the benefits of healing sessions, or counselling sessions. Other therapies could also benefit. If no change is seen in the picture, it means that the basic problem is not being touched, or that the therapist is wrong for the patient, or maybe vice—versa.

How do we interpret the photographs?

As you will be aware 'diagnosis' of illness is the problem area for all medical and complementary therapists. Medical practitioners are being sued for huge amounts of money for giving what the patient saw as a 'wrong diagnosis'.

Common sense often seems to have been forgotten, as in a recent newspaper article which stated that a patient suffering from cancer was attempting to sue his doctor for a large amount of money. The reason was that the doctor had advised the patient that he may only have something like 6 months to live. As that period of time had passed, the patient was consulting his solicitor!

As a healer we must always be very careful what is said to the patient. The code of conduct which healers must obey, states, "Only doctors are allowed to diagnose." Make sure that you follow this directive implicitly!

When I am using the Kirlian camera in conjunction with the spiritual healing, I always make a point to explain to the patient that I have no medical qualifications. I am not a doctor, and I do not attempt to discuss physical symptoms that may affect the human body with them. Not enough research has been done in this area and much more study needs to be accomplished before we can start to interpret the Kirlian pictures, which relate to the physical body.

So, what are we looking for when we have developed the Kirlian photographs?

As I have already stated we have much research to do before we can be confident of our interpretations of the pictures. We are still learning by trial and error, and different people have contrasting views as to what is being revealed. I don't profess to be an expert, but my experiences using an understanding of palmistry, and my own intuition have helped me to be quite accurate in my dealings with patients and clients that I have been involved with.

63

Kirlian Pictures

Picture 22 (page 173) shows my left hand, and the state of my energy level, just after I had arrived in London and visited Guy Mason to take my first Kirlian photographs. Take into consideration that I had, only a couple of weeks prior to this picture being taken, been involved in a car accident. My car had been so damaged it was written off by the insurance company. I walked away with no apparent damage but suffered severe bruising of the chest area but thankfully, after having X-rays, no breakages. But obviously my whole body system was in a state of shock, and I should have taken a rest period to recoup my energy. I didn't do this, which I realise now was foolish of me. I didn't think about it, as to all intents and purposes, I seemed all right. I was determined to go to England to sort out the Kirlian camera, in which I was most interested.

Looking at the picture, note the energy around the thumb area: sheer determination and will power carried me through. A small amount of energy in my (Jupiter) leadership finger shows my ambition was to take the trip. There wasn't much else, was there? Very little energy to speak of. I really was sick, but I wouldn't lie down.

The small (Mercury) finger is showing that psychic/spiritual abilities are still there and the communication aspect also.

The sequence of Pictures 22, 20, 21 and 23 (pages 173, 165, 166 and 174 respectively) show to good effect how the life energy gradually built up in the physical body as my health improved. The hands on healing I was receiving helped me to recover much more quickly than would normally be the case.

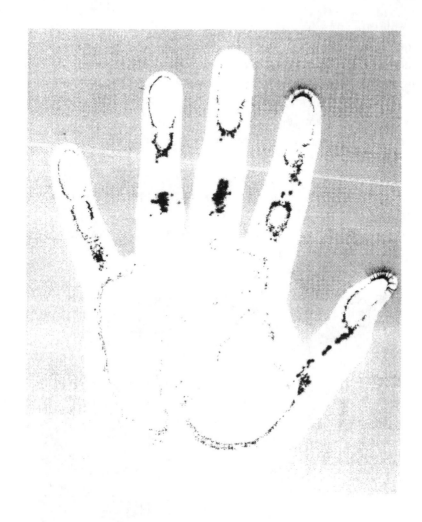

Picture 20. This Kirlian photograph of my left hand was taken a few days later than Picture 22 and shows slightly more energy overall, though still not much to speak of. Again note the thumb (willpower, stubborn attitude). My attention was being focused on the Kirlian camera; it was like Pandora's box being opened. I wasn't really thinking about my state of health, but I should have.

Looking at the picture we can see an increase of the energy in the small finger (Mercury) denoting the fact that I was using my communicating faculty, learning about the camera. We also can see an increase in the index (Jupiter) finger implying that I was seeking out information that would help me. The middle (Saturn) finger also is showing an increase in energy, for I was at last doing something in which I was interested. The ring (Apollo) finger also shows an energy increase and this is the finger denoting creative ideas and abilities. I was becoming more interested and involved in Kirlian photography, and still receiving healing.

The fingers are starting to show increases in energy, indicating that my psychological and emotional aspects are improving by being involved in something that was very interesting to me. My palm area energies are very slowly improving, indicating that my physical body was reacting at a much slower rate.

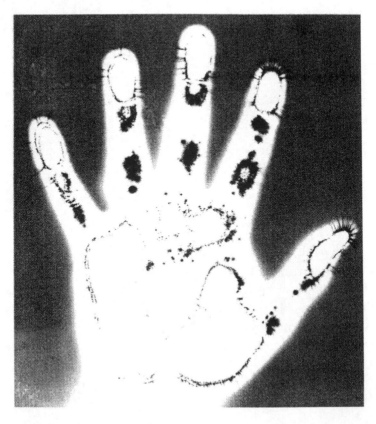

Picture 21, on previous page. I had been in England just over 2 weeks; I had met Guy and June, and spent time with them working with the Kirlian camera, receiving healing and was lodging at a nice bed and breakfast house, quite near the water at Bosham. This was very tranquil and restful. As you can see my energy level was getting better as I was settling down.

Looking at this picture, the next in the series, we can see that more energy is returning to the hand. The palm area is showing a slow build up of energy, indicating that the body functions are slowly improving. An improvement in what it was looking like.

The thumb area is showing more energy, which I feel is indicative of the strength of will that drove me on to research the Kirlian photography.

The index (Jupiter) finger is starting to show more energy due I believe to the fact that the healing I was receiving was working on a mental level; I was also getting involved in learning about Kirlian photography. The fact that I was actually doing experiments with the camera was helping my confidence and I was putting my ideas into action.

The middle (Saturn) finger shows increased energy, due mainly to the fact that I was doing what I wanted to do and enjoying it. I was more balanced and confident.

The ring (Apollo) finger energy is increasing slowly, mainly due to the fact that the artistic and creative part of me was being used; ideas were coming to me.

The small (Mercury) finger: energy again increasing slowly, for I was communicating with Guy about the Kirlian system. My spiritual (Psychic) abilities were also being used.

My health was slowly improving. My mental and spiritual aspects were becoming more balanced, but my physical body aspects were taking longer to get better. I firmly believe the healing was helping me to carry on. Looking at Picture 23, page 174, we can see a big improvement in energy levels in the physical body (the palm area) and also a better result on all the fingers and the thumb.

At this stage I had completed my course with Guy Mason, the man who made the Kirlian Camera. The whole picture is looking better; energy levels are improving, and the brightness of the energy in the hand is quite distinct. I feel I have to bear in mind the fact that I was a very long way from home, staying in a different country, missing family and friends. I shall be very interested to see a picture at a later date, once I am home and have rested and relaxed in familiar surroundings.

Comparisons—Let us take a look at the difference in the energy patterns in picture 22, page 173, and compare this with the energy patterns in picture 23, page 174.

The thumb area shows greater energy levels. Through my determination and will power I had travelled 10,000 miles to achieve my aim. A big increase in energy on my Jupiter finger; my confidence and leadership aspects were being utilised. The increase in the Saturn (middle finger) is noted, as I had now worked with the Kirlian camera and learnt a lot. The Apollo (ring finger) would indicate that I was being creative and more mentally alert. My Mercury (small finger) shows an increase because I was using my psychic and communication abilities.

The healing I had received and the tranquil area where I was living had all helped to restore my energy. The very fact that I had travelled so far and was pleased with the Kirlian camera and its workings also helped to restore my mental and spiritual condition.

Picture 24, page 175: The hand of a Healer

The hand we have photographed here belongs to a man who is a spiritual healer. When we look at the palm area and then the fingers and the thumb we can see that the energy levels are well balanced. The energy pattern on his palm would indicate that the physical body is in good health, with energy flowing freely. The fingers and the thumb are also showing strong energy patterns and could indicate that the emotional and spiritual side of the person are quite harmonious; all in all, a well balanced hand.

Kirlian Pictures taken before and after spiritual healing.

Picture 25, page 176 (before healing).

The hand shows that her energy level is quite strong on a physical level. The thumb area is showing that there is a lot of determination in her make-up.

A) The small finger (Mercury) would seem to indicate what I would take to be lack of contact with other people.

B) The ring finger (Apollo) indicates lack of desire to try new ideas or to be a bit creative in what she is presently doing.

C) The middle finger (Saturn) would appear to indicate that there is inner strength here, but at the moment seems to be a lack of direction.

D) The index finger (Jupiter) shows lack of confidence, ambition and action, of course due to her depressed state.

My overall view is that there is an imbalance, between the physical and mental aspects. The lady looks very tired and washed out and says she feels weak and fed up though, from listening to her in the counselling session, she is quite in touch with things going on around her. The patient in this case is a lady who is 85 years old, quite frail, but also quite vibrant mentally. She has all her faculties working and was, at the time the photographs were being taken, feeling very stressed and seemingly lacking energy.

Picture 26, page 177 (after counselling session and hands on healing). This picture was taken after I had sat down with the lady concerned and discussed with her how she was feeling, her diet, her hobbies and things that gave her pleasure. It was a general counselling session, during which time she was able to outline several things which were troubling her, and some jobs she wanted to do. She talked quite freely and was quite open to receiving spiritual healing.

The healing was given and then another picture (B) was taken, and my following points were observed.

A) Energy levels in the palm area had increased quite markedly.

B) The thumb area shows a slight increase, and this is borne out by her advising me of her intention to get better during our counselling session.

C) The small finger (Mercury) shows a big increase in energy level, probably because the opportunity to communicate and talk to someone about the situation has been a big help to her.

D) The ring finger (Apollo) also shows a big increase in energy, again due to the fact that this lady had decided to take up crocheting and knitting again, something that she had enjoyed and which gave her pleasure, and which would allow her to use her artistic and creative energies. This in turn would help her not to dwell too much on her problem.

E) The middle finger (Saturn) shows an increase also, I believe, due to the fact that she now seems to be looking at her situation a bit differently, after the counselling sessions.

F) The index (Jupiter) finger shows some increase, due I feel to the fact that she is now taking charge a bit more and feels she can help herself to get better.

In conclusion and after some analysis of the situation I can deduce the following:

A) I feel that it was very beneficial for the lady to be able to talk to someone about the situation. I feel that she needed to express her feelings to someone, and this relieved some of the pressure she was under. Having put some positive ideas to her i.e.: crocheting and knitting, changing her diet, she was more positive about the future, because she felt that she was doing something to help herself.

B) The lady was also quite happy to receive healing and did comment that she felt very relaxed and peaceful after the healing session.

The very fact that the pictures show differences in energy levels would suggest that a spiritual healing and counselling session does have a beneficial effect on the patient. For remember, we are not only concerned with the persons physical welfare, but the mental and spiritual side also.

64

Intuition and the Palmistry Aspect

See Picture 27, page 178.

It has been said that "The hand is the visible part of the brain."

Our brain has two parts, the left and right hemisphere. For reasons beyond my understanding, the left brain relates to the right hand, and the right brain to the left hand.

The left brain is associated with the logical, reasoning side of us. Thus the right hand shows the logical side, what we are doing with the abilities we have, and how we are presenting to the world aspects of our nature.

The right brain is associated with the intuitive, inner person: our abilities, the emotional, mental and spiritual side of us. Thus the left hand shows these same abilities that we possess. Abilities such as healing ability, leadership and communication strengths may be prominent.

We need to understand that corresponding fingers on the left and right hands relate to the same abilities or aspects. For example, let us say that the small finger (Mercury), which shows healing abilities, etc., on the left hand shows lots of energy. When the small finger on the right hand shows very little energy, we could deduce that the person has healing ability and could communicate with others but is not using it. One case which comes to mind did show this situation. The lady in question said that she was very interested in healing, but her husband forbade it.

We must be aware that we need to cross-reference several aspects that show on the hands before we make a comment. In other words, see what is showing in the other fingers and slowly build a picture of what the photograph is telling us.

We have spoken with the patient prior to a healing/photo session, and once the picture has been developed, we will then sit with them and take a look at the picture together. It is at this time that your intuition and your inner feelings will come into play.

"The more you do, the better you get," is the key here. Every picture you see will be different, and the experience you gain from seeing all the assorted hand pictures, with their varying energy patterns, will increase your ability to interpret what you are seeing.

Kirlian photography has been known in Russia and the Eastern Block countries for many years now and a great deal of money has been spent on research and development. It would be very interesting to see what developments have taken place in regard to its use in diagnosis in orthodox medicine. Kirlian photography in the Western world is very much in its infancy and there is a great deal of research to be done. Unfortunately this will require large investments of time and money.

The idea of combining palmistry (an ancient science) with Kirlian photography has been advocated by a leading English researcher, who has had much success with his experiments. My own research, small as it is, leads me to believe that we are on the right track. I would say to all readers of this book that much more investigation has to be undertaken before we can draw any firm conclusions. There will be people who will disagree with my findings, and people who will agree. Do remember that every book you read is that person's opinion, in the same way that you have your opinions. I have included diagrams of my understanding of the palmistry point of view, which I hope may be helpful to you.

Picture 27, page 178, shows the hands of a person who is very well balanced and quite happy with herself. Note how similar the energies are in both hands.

The palms relate more to the physical aspect and the fingers and thumb more to the mental, emotional and spiritual aspects of the person.

The left hand relates to what we call the inner person, and shows the inherited characteristics: those we have been born with, our talents and abilities, etc.

The right hand relates to how we are relating to the world, how we are using our abilities.

Should a person be left-handed, the situation is reversed. In a well-adjusted (balanced) person there will be little discernible

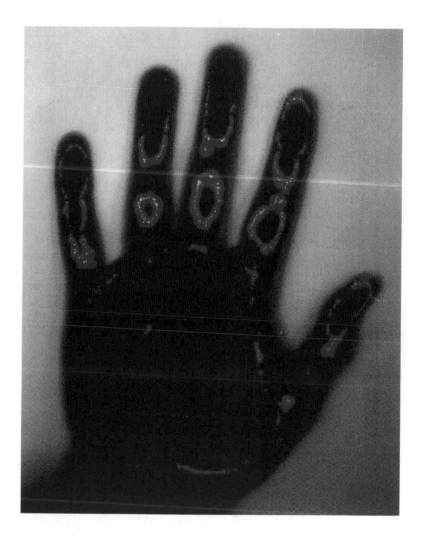

Picture 22. First of four photographs during my trip to London study Kirlian photography, taken two weeks after I had been involved in a car accident. Note the absence of energy in the palm area. The physical body was in a state of shock. Very little showing in the fingers and thumb either.

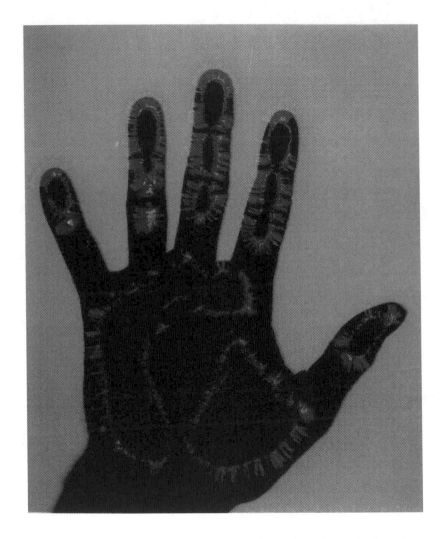

Picture 23. The fourth in the series taken while I was in London. When we compare this picture with the earlier ones we can see that the energy levels have increased dramatically. The spiritual healing I was receiving was definitely having a beneficial effect on me. I was also feeling more settled inside.

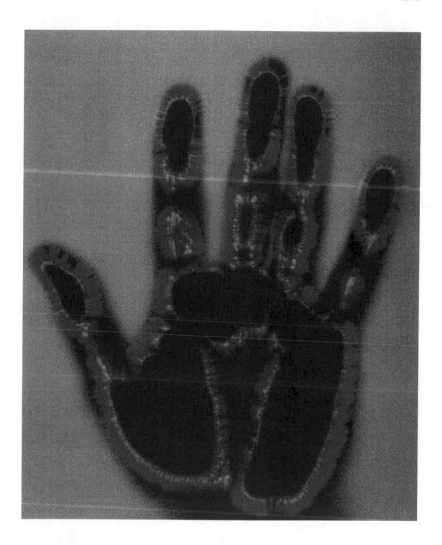

Picture 24. The hand shown here has excellent energy levels, showing a person full of vitality, on both the physical and emotional levels; very well balanced and vibrant. Note the strong energy patterns over the whole hand. It would be very interesting to see the other hand of this person so that we could see if there is a different energy pattern showing. When we have pictures of both hands in front of us we are able to be more analytical.

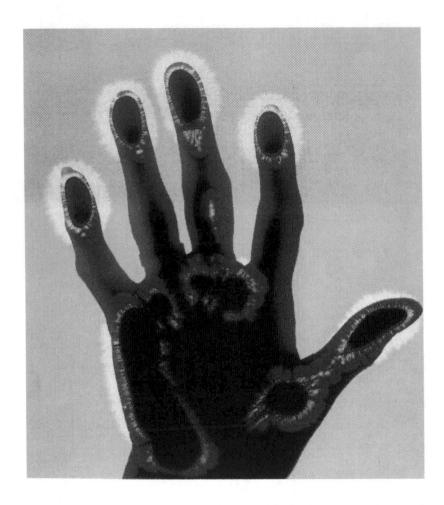

Picture 25. The hand of a mature aged lady showing quite good energy levels despite her age. There may well be arthritis in her fingers which may have affected the photo. When photographs are taken it is imperative that all of the fingers and palm are actually touching the plate of the camera.

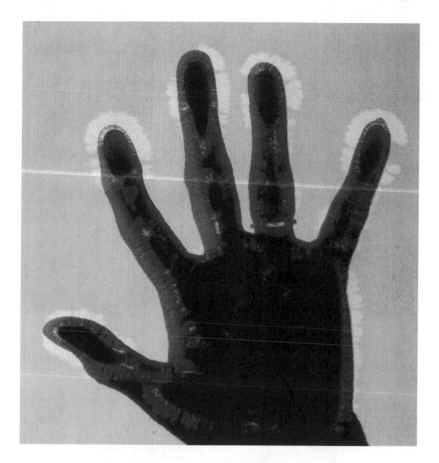

Picture 26. Indications are that the healing session was beneficial to this lady. An increase in energy levels can be seen. In this case I believe the communications session was very good for her. As we become more experienced in healing we understand that many people get a big uplift on an emotional level because during the healing process they get an opportunity to express their feelings. A negative thinking person can receive a boost simply by talking to a person who has a positive outlook on life. Remember—a problem shared is a problem halved.

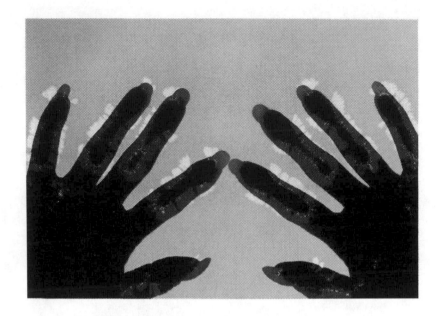

Picture 27. When we analyse a person's hands we need to look at both hands together. I have used this picture to help you to interpret what is shown. This person is well balanced.

Picture 28. Kirlian images of the fingertips aura. Every one of us is different and these pictures show how unique the aura is with each person.

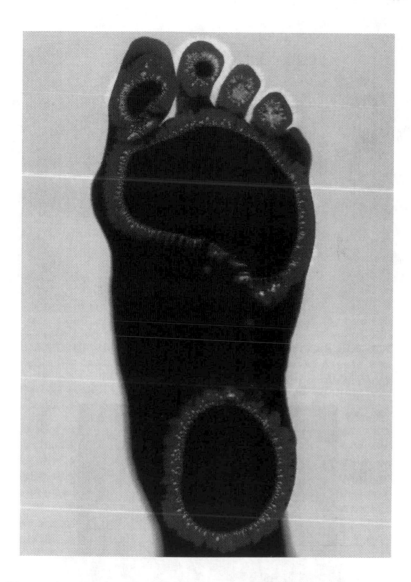

Picture 29. I have included this picture of a lady's foot to show that feet can be photographed in the same way that we can photograph hands. As can be seen in the picture, the foot has quite pronounced energy patterns. It would be most interesting to do research into Kirlian photography of the feet; people who practise reflexology might have some input on the subject.

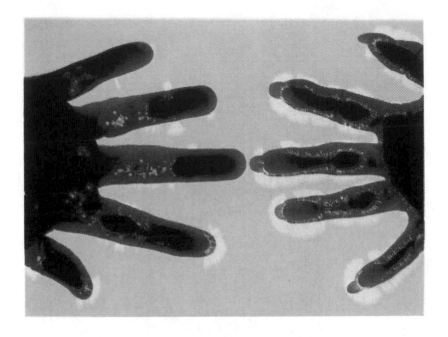

Picture 30. An interesting photograph, something quite unusual. Look at each person's energy patterns. Do men close off, either intentionally or not realising it?

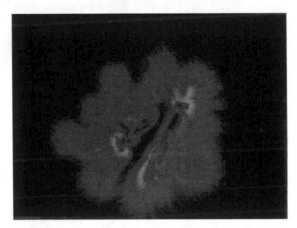

Picture 31. This picture shows that energies can also be seen around physical objects, such as the author's silver ring.

difference in the hands. This is the first thing we look for when interpreting the hands.

The thumb denotes will power, independence, strength of character, confidence energy.

The index (Jupiter) finger denotes leadership abilities, organising ability, and decision making, action and power.

The middle (Saturn) finger appertains to career, job situations, and major directions in life, attitude to life, stability.

The ring (Apollo) finger denotes our creative, artistic side, ideas we have, how we conceive things.

The small (Mercury) finger deals with communication, expression, and interaction with others, counselling and listening skills, and psychic/spiritual abilities.

A stronger energy pattern in the left hand could suggest that the person is sensitive, idealistic, and has difficulty putting their own ideas into operation. A stronger energy pattern in the small finger of the left hand as against the right hand could suggest that the person has mediumistic, healing ability but is not using it.

A stronger energy pattern in the right hand could suggest that the person may be materialistic by nature and ignoring their emotions and feelings.

In all that I have stated I am very much aware that palmistry is an ancient science and as such there is so much to learn. I have tried to offer a few basic ideas for you to think about. One must not jump to quick conclusions, for example by just taking one finger, and what it shows; we must try to look at a broader perspective. This is of course helped by our interaction with the client, and so we are able to build up quite an accurate understanding of that person.

There are many good books on palmistry available which will give you more information on the subject. The ideas I have put forward are of course my own and I'm sure others will also have their own views.

65

Reaction between two People

See Picture 30, page 180.

This Kirlian photograph was taken with a view to seeing the interaction between two people's energy patterns, one person being a man and the other a lady. (The lady's hand is the one with the long fingernails.) I was very interested in what would show in the picture, as I know both people very well. When I look at the photograph I was aware that each of them has what I call 'an area of space' around them. You have heard people say, "keep out of my space," as if to say don't come too close.

I see here the lady who is a very honest, caring, gentle person who is well able to express her emotions. She is extremely friendly, gets on well with people and is able to mix well. The lady is quite artistic and thus adept at expressing feelings openly, and to me this is shown in the hand, by the energy patterns glowing. She is quite happy and at ease with the situation.

Let us now look at the male hand; here we see quite a different picture. The fingertips, which are associated with the emotional state of the person, show no energy patterns, other than a small amount on the index finger. The male had guarded his emotional aspect or withdrawn on an emotional level, most likely not consciously doing so. Looking at the area of energies in the fingers we can see that on a physical level and mental level the energy is there. I know this man is very much in control of his emotions. A very caring person, a healer and a giver, but doesn't like to show emotion. I know there is a strong friendship and understanding between them. It would be interesting to research the photographs of other couples and see what transpires.

66

Conclusion

My idea of putting Kirlian photography and Spiritual Healing together came about because many patients expressed to me the fact that after treatment, be it orthodox medicine or complementary, they were often told that they were improving but didn't really feel as though they were. By taking a Kirlian picture before and after treatment, it is possible to show them that changes in energy levels have taken place. The picture taken after treatment could be done after one session or a series of sessions. Now I understand that some people will say that this doesn't really prove anything and that they may not agree with my methods. I also accept that there needs to be much more research done on the subject before we can say for certain that we are on to something. Research and development is quite expensive and takes time, but I do feel we have to start somewhere, and this is what we, in our small way, have done.

The fact that many people suffer from psychosomatic problems in this day and age does, I believe, offer us an opportunity to use the Kirlian method to assess the situation. Using palmistry to interpret what the Kirlian picture is showing gives us an insight into the person's mental and emotional make-up. Our main concern must be the patient's welfare, and when a patient is able to see for themselves, before their very eyes, their own hand print with the relevant differences showing, it surely gives them confidence.

As I have already said, much more research needs to be done on the subject. There are most likely many other people working with Kirlian apparatus around the world who could, maybe, get a dialogue going with each other to press forward into the future.

In conclusion may I say that any therapy, be it orthodox medicine or complementary, could make use of the Kirlian system to show improvements following treatment, as I have done with spiritual healing.

67

Equipment for Kirlian Photography

I use a Kirlian camera and power unit made by Electro-Imaging in the UK. I am happy to provide information on the supplier.

A DUKA 50 safelight is used in the darkroom, enabling us to see what we are doing in the taking of pictures and in the processing.

The chemicals and paper used are from Ilford Films. The best results have been obtained using Ilford Ilfochrome Classic CPMIM paper, 8 x 10 inch sheets.

I use the Ilford Ilfochrome Classic P 30 system developer, bleach and fixer.

The pictures are processed using an Ilford CAP 40 processor. Excellent results have been obtained.

To contact David or to order your copy of the book please write to

David Clements

PO Box 731

Mirrabooka, WA 6061

Australia